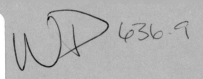

The Professional's Book of Gerbils

KEEPING AND BREEDING GERBILS

Robert Bernhard

The Professional's
Book of Gerbils
TS-120

Photographers: Glen Scott Axelrod, Dr. Herbert R. Axelrod, Paul Bartley, Michael Gilroy, Ray Hanson, Kathleen McGarry, D.G. Robinson Jr., Sally Anne Thompson.

Title page: Although gerbils are not strictly nocturnal creatures, the high temperatures in their natural habitat cause many gerbils to venture from their burrows only at dusk and dawn, when the weather is much cooler.

Distributed in the UNITED STATES to the Pet Trade by T.F.H. Publications, Inc., One T.F.H. Plaza, Neptune City, NJ 07753; distributed in the UNITED STATES to the Bookstore and Library Trade by National Book Network, Inc. 4720 Boston Way, Lanham MD 20706; in CANADA to the Pet Trade by H & L Pet Supplies Inc., 27 Kingston Crescent, Kitchener, Ontario N2B 2T6; Rolf C. Hagen Ltd., 3225 Sartelon Street, Montreal 382 Quebec; in CANADA to the Book Trade by Macmillan of Canada (A Division of Canada Publishing Corporation), 164 Commander Boulevard, Agincourt, Ontario M1S 3C7; in the United Kingdom by T.F.H. Publications, PO Box 15, Waterlooville PO7 6BQ; in AUSTRALIA AND THE SOUTH PACIFIC by T.F.H. (Australia), Pty. Ltd., Box 149, Brookvale 2100 N.S.W., Australia; in NEW ZEALAND by Brooklands Aquarium Ltd. 5 McGiven Drive, New Plymouth, RD1 New Zealand; in SOUTH AFRICA by Multipet Pty. Ltd., P.O. Box 35347, Northway, 4065, South Africa. Published by T.F.H. Publications, Inc.
MANUFACTURED IN THE UNITED STATES OF AMERICA
BY T.F.H. PUBLICATIONS, INC.

KEEPING AND BREEDING
GERBILS

ROBERT
BERNHARD

Gerbils make delightful pets for the young and old alike. Their pleasant personalities make them easy to love.

Contents

Introducing The Gerbil

"Where most hamsters are 'lone wolves' and may be pugnacious, pet gerbils are gentle, amazingly trustful of us humans (perhaps we don't deserve it), and love the company of other gerbils."

A quick glance at gerbils in a pet store might mislead you into thinking they're just overgrown mice — although they do seem cuter and more lovable. Gerbils are rodents all right, and so are mice — but the gerbil's closest relatives are actually hamsters, not mice. Gerbil fanciers contend these critters are far more friendly than hamsters or mice, with a more cheerful and humorous outlook on life.

Where most hamsters are "lone wolves" and may be pugnacious, pet gerbils are gentle, amazingly trustful of us humans (perhaps we don't deserve it), and love the company of other gerbils. Often, they mate for life. They rarely bite, and then only if they're handled roughly or feel threatened. They can become irritable if not fed or housed properly. But above all, they're playful and have an insatiable curiosity about any and all objects and events that can make adults as well as children squeal with delight and wonder.

Some research psychologists think gerbils may be more intelligent than hamsters or your typical laboratory mice or rats (who are pretty clever articles themselves). But sometimes gerbils are so caught up having fun with the lab equipment — ignoring the paces psychologists want to put them through — that they may seem scatterbrained. They just love life.

Another mistake you might make is to assume that such micelike animals couldn't possibly have individual personalities or make friends with humans. You might believe one gerbil behaves just like any other — like cookies cut out by

Note the big, bold eyes and twitching whiskers on this fellow. Gerbils are known for their trusting natures, which make them wonderful pets.

The gerbil is a cheerful, curious little rodent that enjoys exploring the world around him. Each gerbil has its own unique personality, which will be evident to any owner who becomes acquainted with his particular pet.

A quartet of variously colored gerbils. It is agreed that gerbils will do better in captivity if they are provided with a companion.

"As a bonus, gerbils are odorless and as clean as cats, and just about the easiest and least expensive warm-blooded pets to house and feed."

the same cutter — and they may just as well be used in medical research. If you believe all this, you couldn't be more wrong. I'm not going to say gerbils can ever be as intelligent and responsive as dogs or cats, but there's a lot more to these little animals than meets the eye. Children will instinctively understand and enjoy each gerbil's individual personality and amusing ways. Children need only show their pets consideration and not treat them as mere toys. Given care, proper handling, and simple training, gerbils can be a child's friend.

As a bonus, gerbils are odorless and as clean as cats, and just about the easiest and least expensive warm-blooded pets to house and feed. They thrive on pet-store foods and drink almost no water. Their bodies grow to about four inches in length, and their tails add another four inches. Three to four years is a typical lifespan. They do, however, seem to do better if

provided with companionship in the form of a brother, sister or mate. So it's best to buy a pair, or else spend an awful lot of time with your gerbil if it's all alone. With simple preparation you can leave your gerbils for as much as a week while you're on vacation. They're so little trouble that you could even take them with you.

My own children have two gerbil brothers, each with its own distinctive personality. Like all other gerbils, they seem always playful, well-behaved, and curious about anything and everything around them. But they do react differently to situations. One responds quickly to the children and likes being handled. The other is not as anxious to be handled and resists capture — but once its brother is in hand it will follow what the other one does. One is scared of heights and will not venture near the edge of the childrens' beds on which the gerbils sometimes play. The other will readily jump to the floor — but it's scared of the dark cavern under the bed. One guy eats from their little food dish with reasonable table manners for a gerbil. But if the other guy gets there first, he will turn the dish over and then eat the spilled contents. In turning it, he runs from one side to the other, lifting and straining, until he gets the right leverage and over the dish goes. Meanwhile, the more mannerly guy watches patiently and then searches the scattered contents for his meal.

Both of our gerbils talk in various forms of body language as well as through squeaks, chirps, and even stamping their hind legs. And, like most gerbils, both are clever, tireless architects and builders. Offer them some basic building materials — cardboard, cloth, old sweaters — anything they can shred with their chisel-sharp teeth, and they will use their nimble forepaws like human fingers to heap, tug, fluff, and

"Both of our gerbils talk in various forms of body language as well as through squeaks, chirps, and even stamping their hind legs."

One of the gerbil's outstanding characteristics is its long tail, which is usually as long as the animal's body.

A young black gerbil showing a dominant white spot on its head. Several gerbil varieties exhibit this white spot.

"In the wilds, the common household gerbil is a territorial animal. This means they tend to live in one plot of ground and are able to mark the boundaries of their land in various ways that other gerbils can detect."

mold the mess into a desired maze of nests and tunnels. They seem to love to work as much as to play.

But above all they do love their nests and tunnels — a gerbil characteristic I find especially heartwarming. They seem to treasure their quarters and a soft, warmly lined nest, and they are forever redecorating to achieve a cozier design. In the wilds, the common household gerbil is a territorial animal. This means they tend to live in one plot of ground and are able to mark the boundaries of their land in various ways that other gerbils can detect. Other gerbils will usually respect the rights of the landowner, but if they intrude the owner will fight to the death to keep his or her property.

If you don't keep an eye on your gerbils while they are out of their cage, they may turn up in unexpected places.

The hind legs of a gerbil are longer than the front legs. It is not uncommon to see a gerbil standing on its hind legs in order to get a better view of something that arouses its interest.

The next logical question, then, is: Just where do our pet gerbils come from in the first place?

Zoologists estimate there are at least 70 different species of gerbils, all of which are found in dry desert or desertlike areas reaching from South Africa northward to Morocco, Egypt, Arabia, Israel, Iran, and Turkey — and eastward to Russia, India, Pakistan, and Northeastern Asia. The common household gerbil, however, is a particular species from the arid steppes of Mongolia, a country wedged between Siberia on the north and China to the south. The gerbil's Latin name, *Meriones unguiculatus*, doesn't help us much, if at all. *Meriones* was either a warrior in ancient Greece or a war-god in ancient Persia, depending on which authority you read. His distinction was that he wore a battle helmet with boar-tusk decorations. The significance of this in regard to gerbils escapes me as well as other writers.

Meanwhile, *unguiculatus* is a Latin word meaning "clawed." None of this matches the gerbil's gentle nature, although it does have five long black claws on each hind foot. Five toes and only four claws are found on the front feet; the "thumb," if we may call it that, is clawless and looks half-grown. When you see how nimbly it uses those front claws, you may wonder at how similar they are to fingers, including one foreshortened finger, or thumb.

Nowadays, of course, gerbils are bred commercially in many countries. The Mongolian gerbils residing in our homes, however, are descendants of a small stock of twenty that were first shipped to the United States from Asia in 1949, and used only for medical research at that time. They got the job, so to speak, because they were so amiable and easy to keep, and had certain biological characteristics making them

"The common household gerbil. . .is a particular species from the arid steppes of Mongolia, a country wedged between Siberia on the north and China to the south."

These two gerbils are busy checking out their home with their usual activity and nosiness.

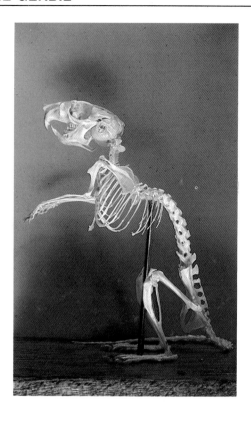

The skeleton of a gerbil. Note the length of the hind legs as compared to that of the forelegs.

"Perhaps the most famous name in modern gerbil history is that of Dr. Victor Schwenkert, who imported the first gerbil shipments to the U.S. in 1949."

animals home as pets. On top of making such nice pets and costing so little to care for, Mongolian gerbils are remarkably healthy animals.

Perhaps the most famous name in modern gerbil history is that of Dr. Victor Schwenkert, who imported the first gerbil shipments to the U.S. in 1949. Before that, Japanese researchers had been studying gerbils in the wilds since 1935. After discovering the Japanese work, Dr. Schwenkert brought the gerbils to his laboratory at Tumblebrook Farm, in Brant Lake, New York. Later, that farm became a leading commercial supplier of gerbils for research labs.

Going back much further in history, we find gerbils should get some credit for one scientist earning a Nobel Prize. In 1892, gerbils were used by the Russian bacteriologist Eli Metchnikoff in his prize-winning research on immunology (the body's defense against disease).

ideal for research in various fields: cancer, neurology, heart disease, endocrinology (study of hormones), drug activity, and parasitic diseases.

What then happened was that scientists and keepers began taking some of these delightful

To come back to gerbils as pets, it's a miracle of nature that these animals are so pleasant and chipper, considering they had their beginnings in one of the toughest neighborhoods in the

Close-up of the gerbil skull. Note the prominent incisors (front teeth) which continue to grow throughout the life of the gerbil.

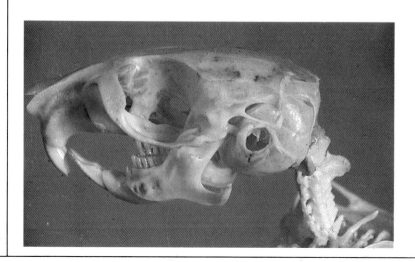

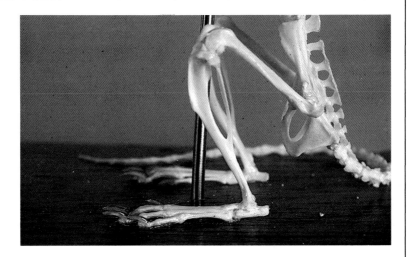

Close-up of the bones of a gerbil's hind feet. The hind feet are longer than the forefeet.

world: the bone-dry plains of Mongolia. The land their ancestors left behind is a treeless plain as far as the eye can see. Situated almost a mile above sea level, it is continually wind-swept, fearfully hot in summer, and fearfully cold in winter. Its wild stretches are home to hawks, fennec foxes, and snakes, which swoop down or spring upon gerbils or small mammals that burrow in the parched sand or dirt among the tough shrubs that survive in practically no moisture the year round.

In this environment, gerbil and burrow have become one. Exposed to predators, the gerbil's natural color is a desert brown — helping to camouflage it from predators — but that isn't enough. The hawks, foxes and snakes are smart and the menace remains. Thus, with no sheltering grass or bushes to hide in, the burrow becomes the only haven. It is also protection against the terrible heat or cold. The burrow is its castle. Without it, no gerbil can survive. But gerbils are territorial creatures, as we mentioned before. Even at the

". . .it's a miracle of nature that these animals are so pleasant and chipper, considering they had their beginnings in one of the toughest neighborhoods in the world: the bone-dry plains of Mongolia."

Close-up of the tail bones of a gerbil. The tail of the gerbil is one of its most interesting characteristics.

A black gerbil looking for something to get his nose into.

Gerbils are wonderful creatures that will bring a bit of sunshine into almost any home.

risk of attack by predators, gerbils chase away any intruding gerbils. Fortunately for gerbils, they have to do very little chasing. They have a gland on their bellies that secretes a smelly substance with which the little animals mark the boundaries of their territory. Usually, therefore, the pungent warning is enough to turn intruders around. The gerbil uses warning signals so that it can stay underground unless it has to look for food. This subject is discussed further in the section on gerbil language, as well as in territorial behavior.

Anyway, wouldn't you expect that, coming from such a harsh place, gerbils would be quite different than they are? Wouldn't you expect them to be jumpy critters, suspicious of everyone's

every move, always on guard, and hiding from flying or creeping enemies? Mongolian gerbils are just the opposite, of course.

In the vast region reaching from southern Africa through the Middle East, Russia, and Asia, many other kinds of gerbils also dig their burrows. But their behavior is less understood and they have not yet been used as pets.

Many species are sometimes called jirds, sand rats or desert mice, as well as gerbils. But all form part of the same subfamily termed the Gerbilinae, which falls within a larger rodent family called the Cricetidae. Gerbilinae, or gerbils, actually means "jerboa-like" animals. Often neighbors of gerbils, jerboas look quite different in many ways. In fact, they hop

"In the vast region reaching from southern Africa through the Middle East, Russia, and Asia, many other kinds of gerbils also dig their burrows. But their behavior is less understood and they have not yet been used as pets."

A pied type gerbil becoming acquainted with a human hand. Once your gerbil becomes used to you, it may actively seek your company.

A pregnant black female gerbil. The area of the abdomen is noticeably rounded.

A wild pygmy gerbil looking out of its burrow. The burrow of a wild gerbil may be covered loosely with sand and small rocks, and it is usually difficult to locate.

"The term cricetids stems from the Slavic word for hamster. So, gerbils are jerboa-like animals belonging with the hamster group."

around on very long thin hind legs, looking rather like mouse-shaped kangaroos with legs that would better fit one of those tall wading birds. Their ratlike tails are easily twice as long as the animal's body. However, gerbils do have longer hind legs than

forelegs, and they sometimes jump or hop like jerboas.

The term cricetids stems from a Slavic word for the hamster. So, gerbils are jerboa-like animals belonging with the hamster group. All cricetids are rodents, and they first appeared on this

A normal or wild type Mongolian gerbil. Most of the gerbils sold in pet shops are Mongolian gerbils.

20

earth between 36 and 58 million years ago during a geologic period called the Tertiary. (Dogs and cats stemmed from mammals that first appeared about 20 million years later.) Biologists call the Tertiary the Age of Mammals; it was the time when modern types of mammals first appeared on earth and proliferated. Theorists believe this development occurred because of the widespread disappearance of dinosaurs, thus allowing the new mammals to blossom forth.

Like all other rodents, gerbils have incisors, or front cutting teeth, that have a chisel shape ideal for gnawing. But their teeth keep growing throughout life, and only ceaseless gnawing keeps their teeth to a manageable size. Imagine the results if a gerbil (or other rodent) had no hard food or other hard substances to gnaw on! Its front teeth would continue growing until the poor creature would be unable to close its jaws and chew — and it would starve to death.

Whatever you may place in their enclosure will be tested first for chewability. Once past this test, gerbils may gnaw it, whether wood, plastic or whatever, and sometimes end up with shapes bearing a startling resemblance to modern abstract sculptures. I wouldn't be surprised if someday someone

"Like all other rodents, gerbils have incisors, or front cutting teeth, that have a chisel shape ideal for gnawing. But their teeth keep growing throughout life, and only ceaseless gnawing keeps their teeth to a manageable size."

Gerbils are capable of jumping, although they are not as talented in this regard as are their close relatives, the jerboas.

A child's stuffed toy may seem suitable for a pet gerbil, but such toys may be stuffed with fibers that are harmful to the gerbil's health. In addition, the chances are that the gerbil will be most interested in gnawing on the toy and in dragging the stuffing all over the place.

"If a gerbil would stand for it, you could examine its upper incisor teeth; you'd find they differ from mice's teeth in possessing a lengthwise groove."

collected these pieces and exhibited them in a museum.

To assure you that gerbils are not mice, we list the following major differences between the two animals. Gerbils burrow, mice don't. Gerbils have gleaming black eyes that are larger and protrude more than those of mice. Gerbils' ear flaps are larger, their heads are shorter and broader and resemble a chipmunk's. Gerbils' hind legs are longer than their forelegs; mice's legs are all the same length. Gerbils differ in that they have a small naked spot near the heels of their otherwise furry hindfeet. Gerbils have long furry tails, often with a dark tuft at the end, whereas mice have hairless tails.

If a gerbil would stand for it, you could examine its upper incisor teeth; you'd find they differ from mice's teeth in possessing a lengthwise groove. Gerbils have two rows of bumps (termed tubercles) on each molar for grinding food, whereas mice have three rows.

Speaking of teeth, gerbils often eat while sitting on their long hind legs, meanwhile surveying the surroundings. Using their forepaws almost like human hands, they will deftly open sunflower seeds — their favorite food — extract the seed, and drop the shells.

In the wilds, Mongolian gerbils and many other species build their burrows close to one another, forming colonies sometimes sheltered by clumps of brush. Some species live alone, but most live in pairs along with their litters. At least one species lives in communal groups, with many gerbils huddling in the same burrow. Practically all types live on

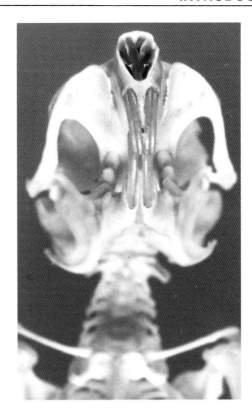

A close-up of the incisors of a gerbil. Note the groove in the center of these teeth. These grooves are not found in mice teeth.

"Speaking of teeth, gerbils often eat while sitting on their long hind legs, meanwhile surveying the surroundings."

Gerbils in captivity need to burrow just as much as their wild counterparts.

Gerbils love to play house. Gerbil houses and other toys are available at your local pet shop.

An albino gerbil climbing its master's hand. Some gerbils will be more resistant to handling than others. Learn to know your pet's likes and dislikes.

typical desert diets of roots, stems, leaves, and whatever fruits or vegetables they can find. Some eat insects as well. Mongolian and other species eat their own feces to obtain B vitamins that are made by bacteria in their intestines. While this sounds repulsive, gerbil feces are odorless, not much larger than bread crumbs, and barely recognizable for what they represent.

"Don't box me in!" Gerbils are very talented at extricating themselves from any situation; therefore, keep an eye on your pet(s) whenever he is out of the cage.

A female may bear up to 15 litters during the first two years of life. Each litter has from one to 12 babies (pups), and the gestation period is 24 to 27 days. Mates may be paired at nine to 12 weeks of age. Many species, including our Mongolian friends, are monogamous in the wilds.

Different gerbil species build different burrows. For example, the 25 species of Moroccan gerbils eke out an existence in short, poorly made burrows dug in shifting desert sands.

A cinnamon white spot male gerbil. Gerbils are experts at getting into and out of tight spaces.

Many gerbils love to run around on beds; if you let yours do so, be sure to watch him so he doesn't run off the edge.

"In India and Sri Lanka, groups of gerbils typically occupy a single extensive burrow. They are reported to catch small birds as well as insects to supplement their seed, root, and vegetable diet."

Since gerbils are creatures of a very dry climate, they are capable of making the most of their food.

Remaining hidden by day, they pop out at night to find insects, seeds or whatever windblown vegetation. They never drink, but get all their water from the fats contained in seeds.

South African pygmy gerbils also make simple desert burrows and emerge at night to eat plants or smaller animals. But when desert plants bloom in the spring, they lay in stocks of seeds and fruit in special chambers set aside in their burrows. The clever creatures build one entrance higher than another to improve ventilation.

In India and Sri Lanka, groups of gerbils typically occupy a single extensive burrow. They are reported to catch small birds as well as insects to supplement their seed, root, and vegetable diet.

Russia's so-called great gerbil is accustomed to snow or hot desert conditions and builds very deep, complex tunnels with crisscrossing paths and many entrances and exits. In some colonies they rarely surface, especially in winter. Some scientists say these animals will stock up to 130 pounds or more of plant material to tide them over the winter.

The fat-tailed gerbil is an odd fellow that ranges from Algeria to Egypt and Arabia. It lives in a simple desert burrow and stores fat in its tail. The tail sometimes gets so fat that the animal can't carry it.

Our Mongolian friends build burrows with many mazelike tunnels, some of which are food storerooms while others are for nesting. The nest is lined with a bedding of chewed leaves. Some observers say these gerbils in the wild are active only at night, whereas others say they're active both day and night. In captivity, they seem to be active just about any time of day or night, the year round. They don't hibernate, as do hamsters.

As you may expect, gerbils are well equipped to cope with the dry conditions and extreme temperature changes of desert life. Chief among the Mongolian gerbil's special equipment is a highly efficient kidney; it conserves water by producing urine that is far more concentrated (contains less water) than in most rodents. (All mammals regulate the amount of body water either by excreting excess water in a highly dilute urine — urine containing lots of water — or by saving water via excretion of a concentrated urine. Urine, which is made by the kidneys, is mainly made of water, potassium, sodium, and urea, which is a waste product of protein metabolism).

Gerbils also conserve water by passing very dry feces. The feces emerge as tiny black pellets.

What this means is that gerbils can get along for very long periods without drinking water. They'll drink if they find it, but they get all the moisture they need from leafy greens or even the high fat content of seeds and grains. The fats are oxidized in the gerbil's body to produce water as well as energy.

Gerbils cope with another major problem for desert-dwellers, which is the loss of water vapor from the lungs as the

"Our Mongolian friends build burrows with many mazelike tunnels, some of which are food storerooms while others are for nesting."

Everything you need for your gerbil's set-up—cage, litter, food—is available at your local pet shop.

An agouti adult with a juvenile light gray and a young cinnamon.

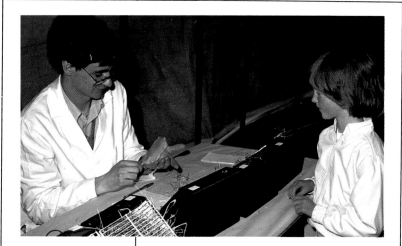

some experiments have indicated that gerbils can tolerate temperatures up to 110° F for about five hours without suffering ill effects. I wouldn't bet on that information, however. Avoid exposing them to direct sunlight for long periods, especially if they're kept in a glass aquarium tank. The glass will act as a greenhouse — and you know how hot it can get in greenhouses. In the wilds, gerbils probably avoid the outdoors during the peak midday heat, and surface from their burrows at dawn or dusk. Their feet are protected from burning sands by dense fur pads, while their bellies which are white reflect heat radiated from the sand.

They have little trouble in the wilds enduring very cold temperatures, as they remain snuggled well below the surface where heat is conserved. Even as pets, they can survive temperatures somewhat below zero for some hours as long as they have a good heap of nesting material to burrow in.

animal exhales with each breath. (Your dog would be in trouble in the desert, as its characteristic panting is used to cool the body, yet rids the animal of precious water.) All gerbils prevent this type of water loss through special bones in the nose. The bones save exhaled water vapor by condensing it into water. The liquid is reabsorbed back into the bloodstream.

As for temperature regulation,

A cinnamon white spot male gerbil. The unique tail of the gerbil helps the animal maintain its balance when it stands on its hind legs.

Choosing Your Gerbils

Opposite: **A cinnamon gerbil. Although many people keep only one gerbil, the animals will be happier if they live with a compatible companion. Gerbils from the same litter generally make good housemates.**

If your mind is made up to buy gerbils, it's best to have everything at hand in terms of housing and other supplies, so the animals suffer the least upset getting into their new quarters and settling in.

The pet store will pack your pets in a secure box that allows sufficient air, but the gerbils will probably be scared by the unfamiliar sounds and smells of the trip home. You'll want to keep them in the box for as little time as possible to keep stress to a minimum. You'd be surprised how stress can make these and other animals more susceptible to infection or other disorders. Whatever arrangements you make, the animals will need a period of adjustment in which they may act more irritable or depressed than normal for them.

An empty tissue box makes a great playground for a pet gerbil.

"Mates that have been split up for as much as three months seem to recognize each other at once when reunited and appear overjoyed."

One Gerbil or More?

Being gregarious and social creatures, gerbils prefer to live in pairs. If you buy more than two, it's best to pair them off in separate quarters. If you're prepared to care for the pups that may result, you may choose to house a male-female pair. Some experts advise choosing gerbil sisters if you want the most harmonious tenants and happiest atmosphere. Sisters are more likely to get along all their lives, including playing with and cleaning each other, and sleeping snuggled up together.

Other pet owners may tell you that they bought brothers, which are as happy as clams. I know this has been true in the case of our own gerbils. At first they had some minor scuffles, but in a few days they settled down to a peaceable life.

I do caution, however, that brothers may get along at first, but then may get on each other's nerves. It's wise to ask pet shop owners what customers are reporting back about their experiences with male or female pairs.

If you do opt for a male-female couple, bear in mind there can be trouble if they become separated for any reason.

They'll mourn for the missing mate, and this could lead to eating disorders, apathy, or irritability. Mates that have been split up for as much as three months seem to recognize each other at once when reunited and appear overjoyed.

Anyway, if you want a male-female couple to raise some pups, you'll do best with a pair that are not closely related and are about 8 or 9 weeks old. At this age the gerbils are not sexually mature, and it's the best time to introduce them. (See chapter on breeding.)

At first, it may be wise to hold your gerbil with your hand wrapped around its body. When it feels more comfortable with you, you can switch to a less severe grip.

A female separated from its mate usually balks at living together with another male. Actually, two sisters may exhibit the same kind of attachment to each other and suffer at the loss of the partner.

Anyway, you'll want to choose young gerbils. Besides watching them grow, you'll be able to train them more easily than older gerbils, and they'll adapt more quickly to their new home. A good age is 6 to 8 weeks, at which time they're quite independent of their mother, as well as robust, not too nervous, and very active. A 4-week old gerbil can also work out very well, but the somewhat older ones just increase the odds of success. Gerbil pups are weaned from their mothers at about 3 weeks, at which time most can eat solid food.

Determining the sex of a gerbil sounds like an easy thing to do. But the problem with young gerbils is that most of them look alike in terms of sex differences. There are two ways that you or a pet store salesperson can decide a gerbil's sex. One is to pick up the animal, hold it upside down, and examine the distance from the anus to the external genital opening; in females it is shorter — about ⅛″ to ¼″ — whereas in males it is more like ½″. A second way is to observe the coloring of the scrotum area (if you think it's a male); in the male the area has darker fur around it.

Sometimes, males may be identified by the shape of their buttocks. Again, holding one upside down, males have more pointed or triangular rear ends, whereas females have more rounded bottoms. A male's bottom also is more tufted.

How do you hold a gerbil upside down? How do you catch and hold a gerbil at all? These questions are answered more fully later on ("Learn how to pick them up," in this chapter). However, pet store and laboratory personnel usually pick them up by the base (not the

Proper living quarters will go a long way towards keeping your gerbil healthy throughout its life.

tip!) of the tail, which makes it easy to hold them upside down. But there are animal lovers who object to this practice either because it seems like an undignified way to treat a pet, or because they believe the tail bone is easily broken this way.

both healthy and have the right attitude for a gerbil.

A healthy gerbil should have a thick, soft, gleaming coat, and a firm well-fleshed body, as well as bright eyes. It should eagerly investigate your hand or any object you offer, and maybe give

"A healthy gerbil should have a thick, soft, gleaming coat, and a firm well-fleshed body, as well as bright eyes. It should eagerly investigate your hand or any object you offer, and maybe give your fingers a tingling but harmless nibble."

Using the tip of the tail could also be trouble, as it may tear away the loose skin covering that part. Not being able to use the tail, of course, is a real handicap when you've got a handful of squirming, wriggling, and very agile gerbils. It's not uncommon to see gerbils with crooked tails, and you wonder how this came about. The usual explanation is that they had their tails injured in a fight with another gerbil. But could it have been caused by picking up the animal by the tail?

Checklist For A Healthy Gerbil

In choosing your gerbils, of course, you'll want ones that are

your fingers a tingling but harmless nibble.

If the gerbil is sleeping, wake it up. (Don't feel sorry for it; after all, you should have the chance to observe your pet-to-be's behavior.) The gerbil should rouse itself quickly and show curiosity. Our gerbils at home are awakened sometimes at night, when there's sudden activity in the childrens' room where the animals live; when the lights go on and they hear voices, out they pop from their tunnels, noses and whiskers vibrating, looking to see what the commotion is all about.

While all this sounds right in theory, it may not always apply in practice. First, some gerbils can be noticeably shy of people, or even timid. Also remember that they are burrowing animals and have an instinctive need to escape to a burrow-like retreat. Lacking this kind of retreat in which to snuggle up and relax, they may not behave with their normal zest and confidence.

Another potential problem is that the trip from the animal breeder or distributor to the pet shop may have worn out the little tykes or got them a bit depressed. That sometimes happens, and it is a familiar problem to breeders.

Sometimes gerbils just get tuckered out. There is not necessarily anything wrong with them if they're too sleepy to stir or if they're just sitting around or sleeping. Like other small mammals, gerbils have a much faster metabolism than larger

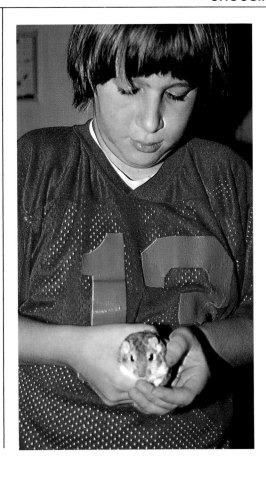

Before bringing your new gerbil home, have the seller show you the proper way to handle it.

"Sometimes gerbils just get tuckered out. There is not necessarily anything wrong with them if they're just too sleepy to stir, or if they're sitting around or sleeping."

After you have had your pet gerbil a while, you will notice that it rearranges the cage to its own liking. Don't be surprised if the food dish and other furnishings are moved on a frequent basis.

Black-eyed white gerbils may sometimes develop a few dark hairs on their tails as they grow older.

Gerbils should be given materials on which they can exercise their claws, as scratching will help wear them down.

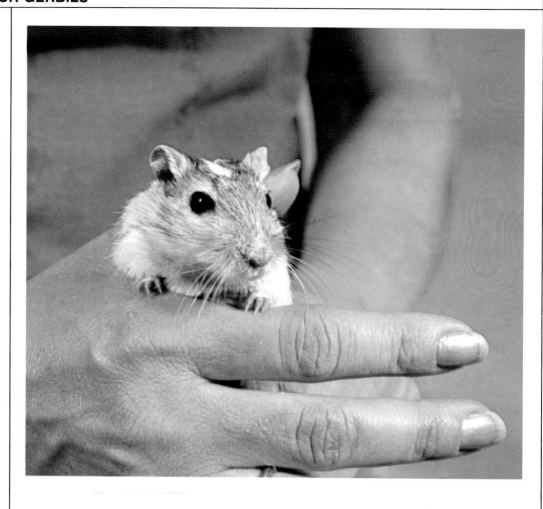

"Something else to think about is that an underweight-looking gerbil is not necessarily sick. It may be the victim of a gerbil bully living in the same cage."

mammals and can store up only tiny amounts of energy compared to larger creatures. So after a period of activity, they get tired just like human babies and need to rest. Most people are astonished to learn that the smaller the animal, the faster the heartbeat and metabolism, and that tiny animals must spend far more time eating. With their speedier functions, they run out of energy more quickly.

Something else to think about is that an underweight-looking gerbil is not necessarily sick. It may be the victim of a gerbil bully living in the same cage. Sometimes a male will push females out of the way at the food dish and the females could have trouble getting enough food.

There's usually an excess of food in the cage, so that's a rare problem. I've seen cases, however, where a gerbil was underweight because every time it picked up something to eat, a mate would slap the food out of its mouth or paws. The mate didn't eat the food, but just seemed to do it for spite, or that was its distorted idea of fun. Nobody says you can't have an oddball who may give other gerbils a bad name.

At any rate, now you can look for signs that the animal may be unhealthy or have a problem you ought to ask about. There are six signs of a possibly unhealthy gerbil (note, I said *possibly*).
1. Sluggish or apathetic behavior.

Healthy gerbils should have thick, clean coats and bright eyes. In addition, they should have an active interest in their surroundings.

Note the bright eyes and clean fur on this fellow. This is an example of a gerbil that would make a wonderful, healthy pet.

". . .the fur may be matted simply because the gerbil has been sleeping all curled up and piled against other gerbils."

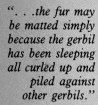

Keep in mind that gerbils may feel ill at ease if they are recent arrivals at the pet shop. In such a situation, one should not expect them to be at their best.

2. Body sores or excessive scratching which could be fleas, mites or other parasites. (Fleas, etc., are very rare, but you never know.) The gerbil may have been in a fight and could be overly aggressive.
3. Symptoms of poor diet, such as shaggy fur, falling fur, bald spots or lameness in the hind legs. Of course, the fur may be matted simply because the gerbil has been sleeping all curled up and piled against other gerbils.
4. Signs of diarrhea, which may be caused by eating wet or decayed food or too many leafy greens. But it may also be caused by an intestinal infection. Check the anus and

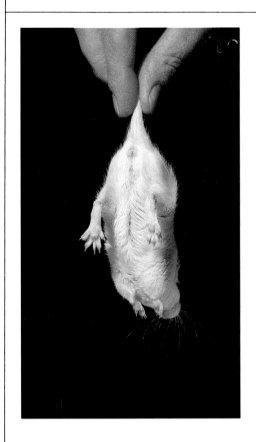

Your pet shop owner may be able to help you determine the sex of your gerbil, and he will most likely be able to show you the proper way to hold a gerbil for this procedure and for others. Keep in mind that a gerbil should never be held by the tip of the tail but only by the base.

Gerbils will play with anything that comes their way. Therefore, it is imperative that they be given only safe toys. In many cases, it is best to offer them the special gerbil toys sold in pet shops.

During handling, the gerbil should be supported in the palm of your hand or by being nestled on the back of one hand and shielded with the other. Never hold the gerbil too tightly.

"Heavy or noisy breathing could mean a respiratory infection. Most likely it's a common cold, but it may be a more serious condition such as pneumonitis (lung inflammation)."

genitals to see if they're smeared with droppings.
5. Eyes are murky or secreting a thick fluid, or lids are swollen. The problem could be infection or allergy. Like humans, gerbils can be allergic to various materials in their environment, such as the wood shavings commonly used

for their bedding.
6. Heavy or noisy breathing could mean a respiratory infection. Most likely it's a common cold, but it may be a more serious condition such as pneumonitis (lung inflammation).

Learn how to pick them up. Don't leave the pet store with

your gerbils until you've asked how to pick up these elusive, nimble-footed animals. You'll have to pick them up sooner or later, not only to play with or train them but to remove them from their cage while it's being cleaned. Keep in mind that although gerbils rarely bite, they may do so if they're frightened by rough handling.

Now that I've planted doubts in your mind about picking gerbils up by the tail, I hate to leave you in limbo about it. All I can say is: Why take a chance if you can help it? If you just can't resist the desire to use the tail, compromise by using your other hand to hold up the gerbil's body.

The simplest approach to capturing a gerbil is to set out a small container — a paper cup or something like that — and lay it on its side. You could also use a hollow tube, such as a toilet paper roll. Odds are that the gerbil will scoot up to sniff and investigate the object, at which point you may be able to push it inside. Then seal the container (on both sides if necessary) with your hand(s). Unload the gerbil onto your hand or into another cage you may be using when you're cleaning the main quarters.

If that doesn't work, try the brute force method of snatching the critter in your hand. One way

"If you just can't resist the desire to use the tail, compromise by using your other hand to hold up the gerbil's body."

You may wish to purchase packaged shavings for your gerbil's cage. Keep an eye on your pet, however, since some gerbils may be allergic to such products.

is to first make a tent out of two hands by interlacing the fingers, as if you were going to twiddle your thumbs. (You could even try twiddling in hopes of throwing the gerbil off guard or distracting it from your real purpose.) Then invert the tent over the gerbil, thus trapping it. Using one hand, slip a thumb under its belly and bring the forefinger around the other side and under the belly. Hold on securely but not tightly. If you have quick reflexes, then like the average child you can use the thumb-and-forefinger grip to gently grab the gerbil even as it's scampering full tilt.

Another method is to slip one or both hands, cupped with palm up, under the gerbil and just lift.

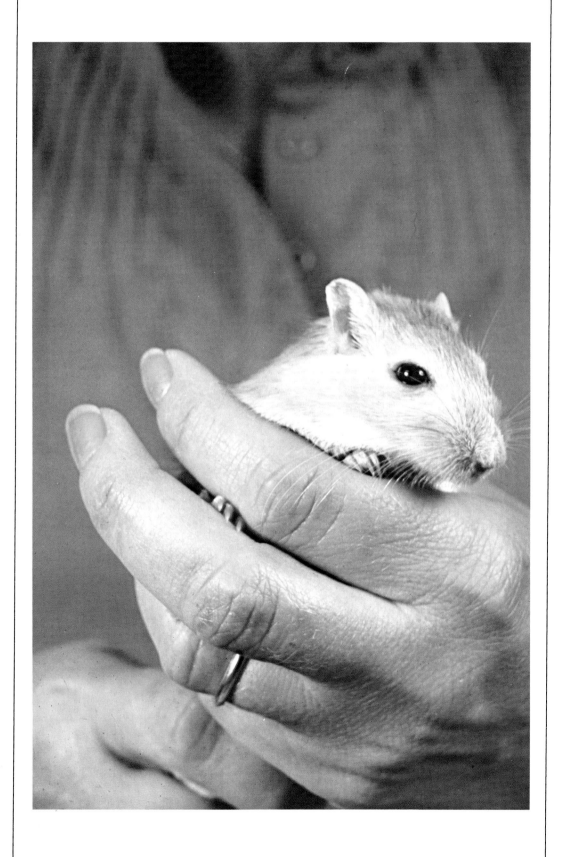

When checking a gerbil for health, be sure to look closely at the ears to make sure they are free from mites and cuts.

Bed and Board

"At least one manufacturer makes plastic cages. . .that come with all kinds of snap-together toys, feeding dishes, watering bottles, horizontal and vertical tunnels, and whatnot. They remind me of the futuristic buildings you might have seen in science-fiction movies."

A Home

Various types of gerbil homes can be bought in pet stores. They include wire-bar cages with solid bottoms, glass fish tanks (aquariums), or plastic terrariums of the kind that some children also use for water creatures they've captured at the shore, ponds, etc. At least one manufacturer makes plastic cages (clear plastic walls) that come with all kinds of snap-together toys, feeding dishes, ladders, watering bottles, horizontal and vertical tunnels, and whatnot. They remind me of the futuristic buildings you might have seen in science-fiction movies.

Each type has good and bad aspects, which are discussed below, but whatever you get, it

Gerbils love tunnels and mazes. Sometimes, however, it may take a more adventurous soul to entice the others to try it out.

Gerbils will most likely decimate any vegetation that is placed in their cage. Therefore, it is probably better to save the green foods for meal times.

Gerbils appreciate play time, whether they remain in their cage or are allowed out. They will enjoy almost any safe toy that they are given.

Be extra careful about what goes into your Christmas stockings! A gerbil will probably find the stocking great eating, not to mention what it would think of the things it will find inside.

Small naked-soled gerbils foraging for food after sundown. These creatures live in the semi-deserts of eastern Africa.

"The noise of chewing on plastic may be worse than anything else."

Many gerbil pairs become inseparable pals and playmates.

has to provide enough space. Enough for a gerbil pair means a floor that is typically 12″ (or 18″) by 20″ (or 24″). High walls, at least 12″ high, are needed to keep the varmints from jumping out but still allowing them to jump when the spirit moves them. For safety, you need a ventilated top or wire mesh, if only to keep out a jealous dog or mischievous cat. Proper mesh covers may be bought at the pet store. Don't use a window screen, which the gerbil can easily chew through. Whatever you get, they'll try to chew it, but some materials will weather the punishment, others will not.

Chewing, in fact, is often a problem with plastic containers and plastic toys (tunnels, wheels, tiny houses, blocks, etc.) If the plastic has an edge, the gerbils will find it and gnaw it to shreds. A worse problem may occur with toys, which the gerbils will soon reduce to shadows of their former selves, or just to plain wreckage. The noise of the chewing on plastic may be worse than anything else. Still, plastic environments remain popular and people have different experiences with them.

An economical and popular residence is a 10-gallon aquarium, which can be gotten at discount if you ask for one that's leaky. If you're in the pet store

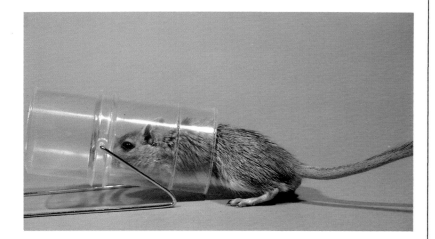

Give your gerbil a tunnel and he'll be off and running.

Gerbils love toys with entrances and exits. They will enjoy furnishings like this for hours.

and overhear a customer asking for five or six leaky tanks, you'll know the tanks are needed for raising lots of small animals or breeding them.

A good point about aquarium tanks is that their walls are solid as well as transparent, thus keeping the bedding or dry food

from spilling out into the surroundings. On the other hand, the bottom is not removable, and so it's a bit harder to clean than enclosures with snap-out or removable bottoms.

There are different opinions about whether the aquarium should use a soft or hard putty to seal the glass joints. Check this out with the pet shop. To my knowledge, modern fish tanks use a silicone sealant, which is as hard as glass. This hard substance may have a lethal effect, some experts contend, even if only minute amounts are gnawed off and swallowed. Soft putty is supposed to be safer in this regard. But so far I haven't heard any reports of this kind of trouble. Anyway, I don't know if soft-putty tanks are available.

Wire-bar cages are popular, although some gerbils have gotten nose sores from repeatedly poking their noses through the bars. Also, think twice about placing an exercise wheel in one of these cages. An alert issued by the U.S. Department of Agriculture warns that a number of gerbils have broken legs by getting hung up between the wheel and the wall bars. I'm not sure how this could happen except in cases where the wheel is very close to a wall; an accident could occur when a

gerbil on the wheel gets a leg trapped between the wheel and wire wall, and the wheel turns — and boom. Perhaps such mishaps may be avoided by setting the wheel in the middle of the cage instead of, as is often done, hanging it from a wall.

The open walls of a wire cage allow bedding and other litter to spill out and get walked all over the house. Some owners solve this problem by getting a box that is lots wider and longer than the cage, and then cutting down the sides to a height of about six inches. They place the cage in the box, and thus keep the litter under control.

Hamster cages are available in the needed size — 14″ by 24″ floor and 10″ high. These cages have horizontal bars, which may appeal to some gerbils who like to climb as much as hamsters do. Don't put two gerbils in the typical small hamster cage, which measures only 8″ by 6″ by 8″ (high).

Another suitable lodging, the plastic terrarium, is available with a 20″ by 14″ floor and 13″ high walls. These enclosures come with slotted covers. They might not be as airy as mesh-covered jobs, in some people's opinion, but I haven't heard of any overheating problems with them.

Make no mistake, however; overheating can be a problem with any home. Ideally, gerbils should have dry air and surrounding temperatures ranging from about 65°F to 70°F if they are to be in tip-top form. It

"Ideally, gerbils should have dry air and surrounding temperatures ranging from about 65°F to 70°F if they are to be in tip-top form."

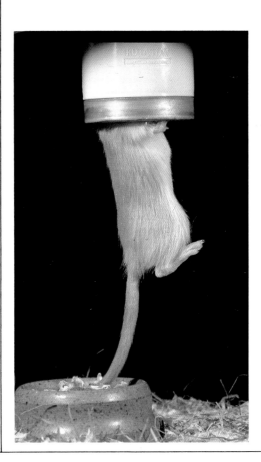

If there is something to be explored, a gerbil will find a way to get in the middle of it.

A mother gerbil peeking out of the tunnel to keep an eye on her six-week-old daughter.

A gray gerbil and an agouti sharing a wooden tunnel.

Watching a gerbil enjoy a tunnel like this will keep the owner entertained for hours upon end.

can easily reach 85°F or more in the summer, which doesn't seem to bother gerbils too much, but they don't excel in that weather. What indeed may be dangerous is to place their cage or tank in direct sunlight outdoors (even indoors) for any length of time. Gerbils could dehydrate or suffer heat prostration in those conditions. Remember, a glass tank is a greenhouse that could reach more than 100°F in a short

time outdoors. If you do take them out in the sun, whether in a tank or not, make sure they have a shady or sheltered place to hide when they feel the need.

Bedding

As long as they can chew it, shred it, fluff it up or push it around, gerbils will mold it to make a nest or burrow. Many owners buy a packaged processed material that looks like wood chips glued into a flat sheet, which the gerbils shred to their liking. Most owners, however, buy packaged, loose wood chips or shavings made from either pine or cedar, or processed corn cob (which looks like the large crumbs left at the bottom of an empty popcorn bucket). Whichever, it should be piled up on the floor of the enclosure to a height of about 4 to 6 inches.

If the gerbils are allergic to any of these materials, they may seem to have a continuing cold they can't seem to shake, or their eyes may swell up. At that point you'll have to try another bedding material, or even go to something as basic as grass hay. But whatever else you put in the

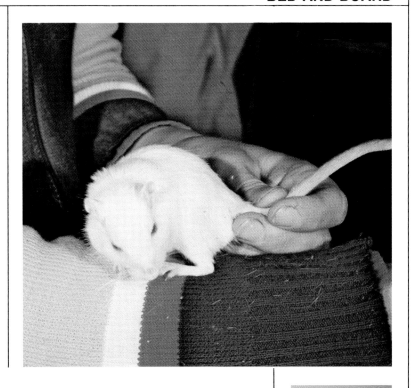

Always take care when handling your gerbil's tail, as it can easily be broken.

"If gerbils are allergic to any of these [bedding] materials, they may seem to have a continuing cold they can't seem to shake, or their eyes may swell up."

Different types of gerbil tank set-ups are available at your local pet shop.

Individual gerbils may have preferences for different types of bedding. You may wish to experiment with these products, which are available at your local pet shop.

". . .gerbils I have known all love to shred cardboard or old clothes — preferably a wool or cotton sweater — and shape their quarters from that or from a mix of different odds and ends."

cage, gerbils I have known all love to shred cardboard or old clothes — preferably a wool or cotton sweater — and shape their quarters from that or a mix of different odds and ends. At one time our gerbils preferred the sleeves of a wool sweater cut into short lengths. For a time, they simply piled these up and slept in the folds. But then they realized the sleeves would make good tunnels. They pushed, pulled, tucked, and chewed, and produced a neat maze of nests. Naturally, they feel the need to periodically remodel their "villa."

The most common approach is to use a foundation of wood chips or corn cobs on which the gerbils build nests from cardboard, cloth, hay or whatever. You could add a small metal box or a tiny toy house, or a flower pot turned on its side. A wooden box would be good, but it won't last too long in the neighborhood of busy gerbil incisors.

If you're willing to put up with a harder cleaning job, fill the enclosure with sand or a sand-dirt mix. You might be lucky enough to actually see how gerbils burrow in their native lands.

Keep It Clean

Because gerbils produce less than a dropperful of urine daily, and their feces are dry and odorless, the bedding need be changed only once every two or three weeks. To show you just how clean gerbils are, they usually save a spot in the cage for their feces. If you find the spot, see what they do if you place

A gerbil sticking its nose out of the "house." Keep an eye on the toys you give your gerbils, as they will probably need replacement after a while. Remember that gerbils will chew on almost anything.

". . .in my experience, water dishes, like food dishes, soon get filled with bedding, food, and whatnot. If not that, then they're promptly turned over."

their food on it. They'll carry it to another part of the cage before eating.

Water

A standard 8-ounce watering bottle should be a fixed part of the gerbil's enclosure. These may be bought at any pet store. The bottle hangs upside down, suspended from a wall by clips. It can't be turned over and, after a short time, the gerbils learn how to get water from it any time they want.

Alternatively, a small watering dish can be placed on the bedding. Some owners prefer this because they claim watering bottles often leak, and often you don't detect the leak until the bedding is wet and the gerbils are sick. If that works for them, fine. But in my experience, water dishes, like food dishes, soon get filled with bedding, food, and whatnot. If not that, then they're promptly turned over. I can't imagine that our gerbil — the one who turns over the food dish — would pass up the chance to upend a water dish.

Make sure, however, that the water tube of the bottle is always

An albino gerbil waiting its turn to explore inside the cup. Be sure that the gerbil cage does not become overcrowded with toys.

Gerbils are active, inquisitive animals that should be provided with safe toys that will help them exercise their minds and muscles.

A family of gerbils shredding paper towel for a nest. This particular container is overcrowded, a condition which is detrimental to the health of your gerbils.

"Gerbils do need toys, maybe more to entertain us than them — but they seem happier with things to snoop around and crawl over."

accessible and not buried in the bedding. A buried tube is a frequent problem and can lead to trouble if you forget to check the bottle every few days or if you go away on vacation. Gerbils can get seriously dehydrated, even though they don't need much more than a thimble-full of water daily. They may need more if their diet is mainly the dry pellets sold in pet stores.

For a gerbil pair, an 8-ounce bottle of water easily lasts a week. However, many owners change the water daily. Always keep alert for leaks in the bottle. Very slight leaks may be detected only by observing moist bedding around the watering tube. Besides the mess it makes, moist bedding may develop fungus growths that could cause

respiratory infection or allergic reactions in your pets, or even cause allergic problems in pet owners.

You could dispense with water bottles or dishes entirely if you supply lots of leafy greens — lettuce and such — from which gerbils in the wilds normally get their water. Some gerbils, including our own, never touch the stuff and won't eat fruit either.

Toys

Gerbils do need toys, maybe more to entertain *us* than *them* — but they seem happier with things to snoop around and crawl over. Watch how they perk up when you furnish a previously barren cage with toilet paper rolls, "curiosity cubes" (blocks

Although some dogs may learn to tolerate and even like the pet gerbils, never leave the animals alone together.

A homemade gerbil cage containing a fluffy heap of burlap which was laboriously shredded and piled up by two gerbils. For the most part, homemade gerbil cages are inadequate; your best bet is to buy a commercial cage from your local pet shop.

sold in pet stores), tiny doghouse-like items, a plastic shoe, or a gerbil alltime favorite — an empty facial-tissue box. You may also offer them a wheel, but it's the sort of thing that appeals more to hamsters than to gerbils.

Pet stores offer a line of plastic toys. Just be prepared for the

the other, tunneling under the bed clothes, running up to the edge and peering over. As I said before, one of our little guys would never jump down. In fact, most gerbils are afraid of heights. But the other guy will leap at the first opportunity and scurry around the children's toys that

Once again, wire exercise wheels should never be given to gerbils, as the animal can easily catch his tail in the spokes. The only type of wheel that is safe is a solid one which is specially designed for gerbils.

"Our gerbils seem to enjoy nothing as much as romping across a bed, from one corner to the other, tunneling under the bed clothes, running up to the edge and peering over."

inevitable outcome: gerbils enjoy zipping in, out, and around these play devices — but they'll soon wreck them with their gnawing. A good idea might be to lay the toys aside for the times you let the gerbils play on the floor or on a bed.

Our gerbils seem to enjoy nothing as much as romping across a bed, from one corner to

may be scattered on the floor. He'll run up to see what's under the beds — raising up on his haunches in a characteristic gerbil posture and sniffing in the scene — but never enter the vast darkness before him.

Letting them go on the floor, you may have your hands full collecting them again. Make sure the door to the room is closed

Gerbil climbing to the summit of his wooden tunnel house.

The long tail of the gerbil will come off if the animal is attacked from behind by a predator. This is, however, very painful for the gerbil, and the pet owner should take care never to injure the gerbil's tail.

A gerbil-sized bucket is another possible favorite for your pet.

"Dogs can get very jealous when you handle or hold a gerbil. . .A dog's jealousy may overcome its strong sense of right or wrong. . ."

Some gerbils may learn to recognize their owner's voice or the sound of their names.

and beware of the family dog or cat who could take a swipe or snap at them.

Dogs can get very jealous when you handle or hold a gerbil (or any other creature for that matter). A dog's jealousy may overcome its strong sense of right and wrong and cause it to snap at the gerbil in your hand. Even a mild snap — not a real bite — could be disastrous. Once, my wife was holding one of the gerbils and letting our big female dog "BJ" sniff at it. We felt there would be no trouble, as BJ never bothered the gerbils as they played on the floor or wherever — and, anyway, all her instincts seemed focused on protecting everyone in the house, our cats and pets as well as us people. But my wife turned her

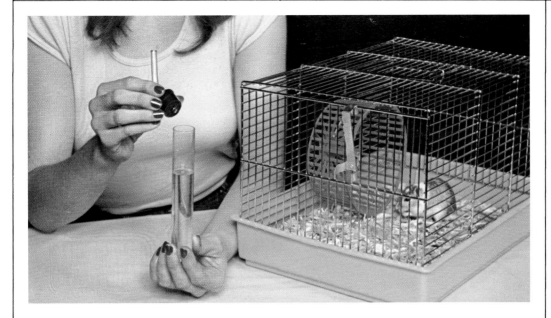

head momentarily, and that's all it took. Snap! BJ narrowly missed, either by design or bad aim. Apparently, holding the gerbil was just too much for BJ to take. My wife had crossed a line BJ had drawn according to her understanding of what makes for an orderly household. In such a house, everything has its place. Cats could go on beds because they were small and neat, and gerbils could go on beds or scamper on the floors because...well, because they're part of the family now. But gerbils in her mistress' hand? That's going too far and deserves either a stern warning — a harmless but frightening snap — or something worse.

Getting back to toys and

"Cats could go on beds because they were small and neat, and gerbils could go on beds and scamper on the floors because...well, because they're part of the family now."

The water bottle should be securely attached to the side of the cage. In addition, the owner should see that all the gerbils learn how to drink from their particular water vessel.

If you don't keep an eye on your gerbils, you'll never know where they will turn up next! Your pet can show up inside a box . . .

playing: Children and gerbils can have a good time playing with building blocks set up on a table or the floor. You can build houses, tunnels, and such, and watch the gerbils do their thing with the constructions. A large dollhouse would be fun for gerbils, but they might chew some valuable or treasured pieces, and you could have problems getting them out when you want them out.

. . . poking his head out of a paper bag . . .

. . . or sticking his nose out of an improvised tunnel!

Cardboard cartons can be fun. Cut doors or windows in the walls, or construct mazes inside them using toy blocks or pasting down cardboard walls. Try teaching the gerbils to run the maze and find food at the end. This is done by letting the little guys find their way to the exit trial-and-error, and getting their food reward at the end. Put them in the maze repeatedly until they know immediately which turn to

A black female gerbil.

A dove gerbil and a white (albino) gerbil.

A cinnamon white spot and an agouti.

Opposite: A gerbil eating out of its master's hand. Gerbils do not bite unless they are badly provoked.

take at every crossroad. The steady improvement the animals show, as measured by how long it takes them to get to the exit, is called the "learning curve."

(Every animal, including us humans, exhibits a learning curve for many different types of educational experiences. Repeated trials at a given task typically result in improved performance, which is slow at first and then suddenly speeds up.) Anyway, good luck! Gerbils are poor performers in maze experiments because, research psychologists tell us, the animals

just can't get too excited over the reward. They'd rather explore the maze. Now, laboratory mice and rats are whiz kids at mazes. They even outperform humans at comparable maze-learning tasks. Mice and rats are very dedicated to striving for rewards and do not have the same curiosity as gerbils. For gerbils, in other words, nothing seems to be beside the point; everything is interesting. Think about that for a moment. One of the unique characteristics of human beings is precisely their tendency to stray from the point at hand, the

Fruits and vegetables are good sources of nutrition and water for gerbils. However, not all gerbils are willing to eat vegetation— some will avoid it at all costs.

Sunflower seeds are often gerbil favorites; however, too many of them can cause your pet to become obese.

Commercially prepared gerbil food is nutritionally balanced to meet the needs of pet gerbils. You may, however, wish to supplement this diet with other types of food.

"Gerbils will do well on almost anything you'd feed to a hamster — but not to a bird!"

very trait that leads to daydreaming or creative thinking.

Proper Diet

Gerbils will do well on almost anything you'd feed to a hamster — but not to a bird! An adequate diet is usually provided by the pellet-form foods you can buy in pet stores. The pellets commonly contain a mix of grains, including wheat, corn, barley, seeds, and sometimes various kinds of processed fish. Make sure you apply a "label test" to whatever preparation you buy. The label, which is required by the U.S. Department of Agriculture, lists the quantities of protein, fat, etc. in the feed.

The label should indicate at least 20 to 24% protein, and not more than 16% fat. Birdseed has much less protein, usually not more than 10 or 12%.

About one tablespoon of dry food daily per gerbil is a good rule. Offer it once a day, in the morning is a good time, and you can see later on just how much they eat. You'll want to avoid leftovers that can spoil or get moldy. Overeating is not typical of gerbils, unless they get their chops on sunflower seeds. These seeds are fine for gerbils, but they're mostly fat. Gerbils need a low fat diet, which is what they get in the wilds. If a gerbil stuffs itself on sunflower seeds, it will not get the protein it needs from

In the wild, some gerbils may eat insects. In captivity, however, a commercial diet supplemented with fresh fruits and vegetables is best.

"Many gerbils hoard food, storing it somewhere in one of their nests."

A proper diet is especially important to young gerbils, as nutritious food will ensure proper growth.

the dry food preparations.

The dry foods ought to be supplemented by fresh fruits or vegetables, including lettuce, carrots, celery, cabbage, tomatoes, apples, oranges, corn cobs. They also like peanuts, dandelions, popcorn, dog biscuits or other dry dog or cat foods,

pretzel sticks, or potato chips. One thing they can't do is crack hard shells.

Many gerbils hoard food, storing it somewhere in one of their nests. One of our gerbils hoards corn. He removes kernels, one by one, disappears into his sweater-burrow, and emerges in a few seconds to get another kernel. After carting away four or five kernels, he sits quietly for a few minutes, perhaps wondering why he did this work. After all, he's not in the wilds as were his ancestors who needed to store food over the dreadful winters. Unable to carry this thought any further, he blinks and goes on about his daily business.

No matter how you serve the dry food, it will get strewn all over. But a small dish may help keep it in one place and make it easier to remove uneaten victuals. Many owners spike the food and water with vitamin drops you can buy in pet stores.

Try to give them food and water at the same time each day, if only to be sure you don't overlook rotting food or water leaks. It's also a nice chore for children, to get them used to a regular and important responsibility.

If you're going on vacation, better not leave the gerbils for more than a week. Enough food can be left in the dish or on the bedding, and an 8-ounce water bottle will certainly be enough. Something has to be done to avoid the water tube from being buried. One way is to just rebend the metal holder so the bottle hangs higher on the enclosure wall. Cage enclosures present less of a problem, as they allow you to hang the bottle outside the cage and insert the tube higher on the wall.

Some researchers report that even on a dry diet, gerbils can go without water for several months. I don't know if I'd want to take a chance on the reliability of that claim. The report is based on experiments with Indian gerbils, whereas yours, of course, are Mongolian gerbils that may have very different water requirements.

"Some researchers report that even on a dry diet, gerbils can go without water for several months."

Head study of a healthy-looking, well-fed gerbil.

Gerbil Language

"The loudest noise gerbils may make is sort of a drum roll produced by thumping their hind legs."

A gerbil in the act of marking territory with its scent gland. In the wild, gerbils delineate boundaries and will fight to the death over their homesteads.

Before learning how to handle and train your gerbils, it might be helpful as well as fascinating to consider how gerbils communicate with one another. (You can skip this chapter and come back to it some other time if you want.) One always wonders if there were some way we could understand an animal's language enough to somehow mimic their "speech" and have them understand us better — or us understand *them* better.

The loudest noise gerbils may make is sort of a drum roll produced by thumping their hind legs. Now, rabbits are famous for communicating with one another through leg thumping. Remember the famous novel about rabbits in which they thump signals

A black gerbil and a pied white spot gerbil.

"Gerbils' squeaks are very soft and seem more important to newborn pups as calls to mommy gerbil for food or help."

warning of danger over long distances. Some rabbit owners even name their pets "Thumper."

Gerbils' squeaks are very soft and seem more important to newborn pups as calls to mommy gerbil for food or help. Gerbils' main way of communicating appears to be body language — various postures or gestures to express a feeling or viewpoint — or through an odor they emit from that special gland on the abdomen.

Thumping

Thumping has at least two meanings for gerbils. *They* can tell the different messages apart, but so far *we* can't.

When pursuing females for the purpose of mating, males will sometimes stop long enough to give some good thumps — and then continue with their original intentions. Gerbils will do this either in the wilds or in captivity.

But in the wilds, thumping also is used to signal danger to other

"Gerbil pups have been observed repeating their parents' thumping without the presence of danger or mating behavior."

gerbils in a colony, as well as tell another gerbil it wishes to mate. Sitting up and scanning the desert landscape and sniffing the air, they'll drum loudly if they spy danger in the form of suspicious shapes, sounds or odors. They flee into their burrows, while other members of the colony appear to be alerted and also go underground.

Gerbil pups have been observed repeating their parents' thumping without the presence of danger or mating behavior. This may be taken as evidence, however slim, that parents teach thumping to their offspring. In other words, it's not something gerbils inherit from their parents. On the other hand, the parents would have an instinct (inherited from *their* parents) to

teach pups thumping, while pups also would have an instinct to repeat their parents' behavior.

Body language is used commonly among pet gerbils. The following is a "dictionary" of body-language words.

Greeting. Almost looks as if two gerbils are kissing; they lick each other's mouth.

Happy or *tranquil.* Like cats, they wash their face, belly, and back at a leisurely pace, and clean the tail while holding it in the paws.

High spirits. Jumping with all four legs off the ground at once — sometimes called "flea jumping" — or playful boxing with the forepaws. The boxing may look like a scuffle, which it sometimes is.

Fear. Sitting upright in a frozen

Like people, gerbils communicate through body language. If you get acquainted with your gerbil, you will learn which signs mean what.

A pair of gerbils greeting each other. This greeting looks just like a kiss hello.

Learning to read the gerbil's body language will help the owner determine the best time for handling his pet.

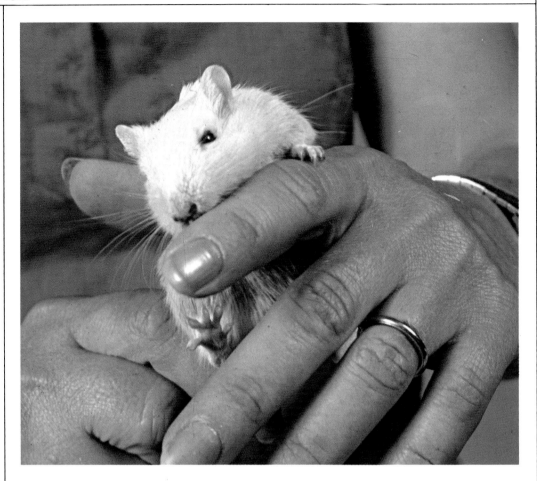

"The annoyed gerbil rejects another gerbil by pushing at it with the head."

This gerbil is certainly curious about something. Note the way it is sniffing the air.

posture, with forepaws clenched and held close together as if praying.

Curiosity. As in fear, but the gerbil seems relaxed, sniffing the air with twitching nose and whiskers and bobbing its head.

Inviting a mate to groom. The body position is similar to the gyrations cats go through when they're signifying "surrender" or let's be friends or play: the gerbil lies on its back in front of the other gerbil, and twists its head back to expose the throat. Females wolves expose their throat this way to indicate submission to the pack's dominant males.

Go away, don't bother me. The annoyed gerbil rejects another gerbil by pushing at it with the head.

About to fight. Two gerbils about to scuffle may push with their heads while in a head-to-head position.

Odor Marks Its Territory

Like so many other territorial animals, gerbils have a way to warn other gerbils they are trespassing on private property and had better leave or else.

Male gerbils mark the boundaries of their territory by rubbing their belly over the ground. This leaves an odor of the secretion (sebum) that's produced in the special gland. The gland is a hairless organ in the skin about ½″ in diameter and located in the middle of the abdomen. In adult males it may have an orange color. The

The ability of gerbils to use their hind legs as a primary means of support has led many people to call them "kangaroo rats."

If they are properly maintained from the very start of life, your gerbils will live longer and will feel better about the world around them than those animals that have received indifferent treatment.

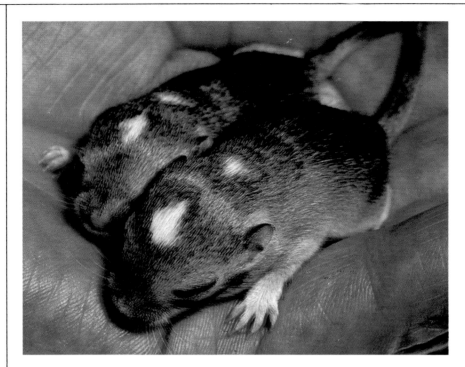

process of marking its territory is known as "skimming." As mentioned in Chapter One, skimming allows the gerbil to warn off intruding gerbils and thus defend territory without exposing itself to predatory animals.

Females also have a scent gland, but they appear to use it for marking territory only when nursing a new litter. At that time, she is far more aggressive than usual and will drive off intruders. Her own pups are marked, which helps her find and

"Females also have a scent gland, but they appear to use it for marking territory only when nursing a new litter."

A light dove gerbil and a cinnamon gerbil. Keep an eye on the gerbils, as they will occasionally (but not often) fight.

Gerbils do not make quintessential maze animals—not because they're not smart enough, but because they are too curious and tend to go their own way.

"Like other territorial animals, gerbils usually respect another gerbil's boundary marks, and they will detour around someone else's property."

Sunflower seeds probably make the best hand-feeding food for your gerbil.

distinguish them from another female's pups if they've wandered off. When experimenters smeared a female's sebum on another female's pups, she treated the pups like her own. Normally, another female's pups would be chased from the nest.

Like other territorial animals, gerbils usually respect another gerbil's boundary marks, and they will detour around someone else's property. This instinct is so strong that when a male is shipped to a new territory where no other gerbils have lived, it will avoid the bedding material that was marked by another male and placed in the new territory.

Male gerbils do fight, however, over who has claim to a previously unmarked territory. The loser may be so crushed in spirit that it may grieve and die, never mating.

In these respects, gerbils are similar to other mammals who use a gland secretion to draw a fence around their territory. Badgers, for example, use a gland at the base of the tail. It's even reported that tame badgers will greet their masters by stamping

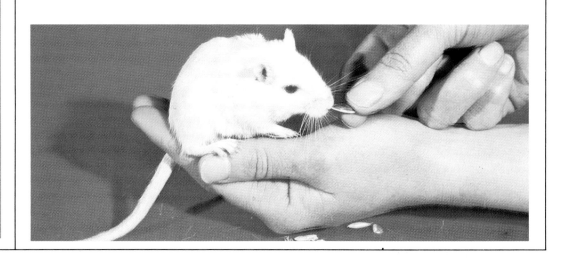

their odor on the toes of his or her shoes. Another well-known example is the male chamois (a kind of antelope); it has two glands behind the horns that swell up at breeding time and release a substance the animal spreads on foliage surrounding its territory.

Why, you may ask, do gerbils need to defend their territory against their own kind? One answer is this: A gerbil's territory, just like its burrow, is its lifeblood. Vulnerable to predators and with few hiding places, they can't stay out in the open for a long time while they seek food. Each gerbil pair needs a relatively small territory in which it knows every root or stem, every seed-pile, and every hole down which it can disappear in a twinkling. It must own all of this, lock, stock, and barrel. The desert, after all, is lean pickings and offers few safe shelters. Gerbils must spread out to make sure each has enough area of its own to support life.

Despite these adaptations to a harsh life, gerbils are eaten in great numbers by desert predators. A key to the survival of gerbils over all the millions of years is that they reproduce quickly and in large numbers to constantly restore their population.

"Each gerbil pair needs a relatively small territory in which it knows every root or stem, every seed-pile, and every hole down which it can disappear in a twinkling."

A trio of differently colored gerbils. Some gerbils will become inseparable, while others will merely tolerate each other.

A golden gerbil who has probably just knocked over his dinner and is looking at the appealing mess on the floor.

Gerbils have a body language all their own. This little fellow is the picture of curiosity, as demonstrated by his alert upright posture and tightly clenched paws.

A dove gerbil and a cinnamon gerbil playing house. Although gerbils will share toys most of the time, they will sometimes fight over a favorite.

Training

You don't have to know any great secrets to tame or train your gerbils. But nothing will work very well unless you handle them regularly while they're young, and remain patient and gentle.

What is in your favor is that, unlike most other animals, gerbils will consider your hand either a pleasant object or certainly a material to explore. Rarely, however, will they volunteer to be picked up at the beginning. A completely tame gerbil will let you pick it up, may even ask to be picked up by running eagerly onto your hand. It likes to be stroked and has lost all fear. A food-tame gerbil will take food from your hand or come out to greet you when you appear or tap on the enclosure, or even talk to it. (It doesn't matter what you say, of course, as long as you

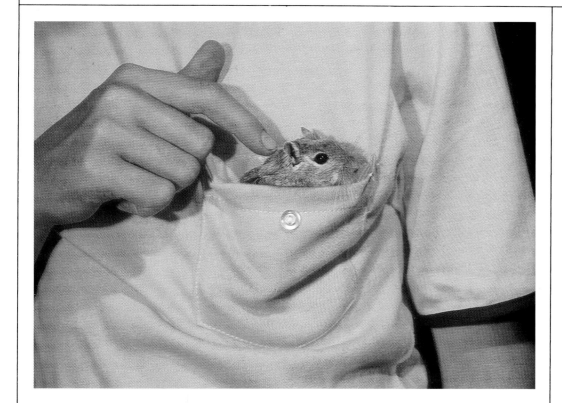

A tame gerbil may love to play inside a pocket without having been trained for such behavior. Beware of the gerbil who likes to chew on clothes, however.

"Keep training sessions short, as gerbils clearly have a short attention span and like to move on to the next project once they've sized up the present one."

don't shout or speak angrily and the animal gets used to your voice.)

Some gerbils actually appear to respond to their name. They'll scurry toward you when you call, and they may sit up and appear to be listening to your words of wisdom or sweet tones. Some may climb onto your hand or lap. A favorite place to go is up your sleeve. Animals that climb around a familiar person show that they are at ease and feel safe. Only when this happens can you truly get to know your gerbils as individuals, not merely playthings or toys.

The first rule is: Keep training sessions short, as gerbils clearly have a short attention span and like to move on to the next project once they've sized up the present one. Also, avoid training during the animal's rest periods. Take a few days to observe your gerbil's activity cycle — when they race around, when they sit quietly, when they go "underground," etc.

Start your training program at feeding time, when they're hungry. You can use food as a reward for good performance. Offer the gerbil some sunflower seeds or dry food, lettuce, or whatever. In most cases, they'll

During handling, the gerbil should be supported in the palm of your hand or by being nestled on the back of one hand and shielded with the other. Never hold the gerbil too tightly.

Lettuce is a good training food. Many gerbils like it, and it provides them with a good source of water.

come and take it from you. Seed would be their favorite, but they'll carry it off and you won't be able to accomplish what you set out to do: pet the head, ears or back with your finger. Lettuce may be better, as you can hold it while the gerbil eats, thus holding it within petting distance. Where there's one piece of lettuce and two gerbils, you may see a tug-of-war between them for possession. This can be a pain. Even if you hold out different pieces of lettuce, one gerbil may very well decide he or she wants the one the other is chewing. Some gerbils are that way. If one is making a pest of itself, remove the varmint for a short time while you tame the other. Then bring the other one back.

(While you're petting a gerbil that's eating lettuce, you might

"Where there's one piece of lettuce and two gerbils, you may see a tug-of-war between them for possession."

Many owners feed their gerbils lettuce in this way. When doing so, be sure that one gerbil does not push the other away or steal from it.

Appealing to a gerbil's curiosity is the best way to have it perform for you.

observe just how they do this, and it will also teach you how they shred cardboard. Sitting on their hind legs, they use their incisors to stitch a line of holes along an edge until a thin strip comes loose. If it's lettuce, they chew the strip; if paper, they let it fall into the growing pile.)

The next time they come out to eat, entice them by calling their name, and give them some food. Pick them up and hold them for a while or play with them inside or outside the enclosure. Use their names as often as possible. One of our gerbils does not respond to its name ("Mugsy") but generally comes when I snap my fingers. The response to finger-snapping came about when I tried to see how it would respond to

The behavior of swinging overhead is common for gerbils who have access to something to swing upon.

"One of our gerbils does not respond to its name. . .but generally comes when I snap my fingers."

Some gerbils will enjoy a ride on their owners' shoulders.

thumping. But while I was
thumping and calling it, I was
unconsciously snapping my
fingers. The finger-snapping got
through, but nothing else. Every
time Mugsy came over I gave him
some sunflower seeds. So the
finger-snapping sank in.

With patience and persistence,
food rewards may be used to
train them to jump on objects or
go through tunnels. Place them
on the object or push them
through a cardboard tube until,
when they do it on their own, you
give them some sunflower seeds.

A word about biting. Gerbils
sometimes bite. But even when
they're scared, the bite is rarely
hard enough to break the skin.
Naturally, a bite that does break
the skin should be washed with
antiseptic and seen by a doctor.
Treatment may be needed to
prevent tetanus. Rabies caused
by a gerbil bite has never been
reported to my knowledge. Don't
take my word for it, however;
check with your state board of
health and local health
authorities, which keep records
of rabies outbreaks. A doctor may
insist the animal be tested for
rabies.

Gerbils often take a nip out of
an offered finger or nibble at you

or your clothes. It's harmless and
nothing to worry about, except it
might startle you if you're not
prepared. While on your lap or in
one of your pockets, a gerbil may
gnaw a hole through your clothes
if you don't pay attention and put
a stop to it. Recently, Mugsy
chewed a hole in my wife's
dungarees while the little guy
was on her lap. She didn't realize
what was happening until the
chisel choppers touched bare
skin.

If your gerbil attempts to escape from you, do not grab it by the tail. Tail injuries are dangerous and extremely painful.

Opposite: Your patience and good care will be rewarded with a friendly, lovable gerbil—a pet you can be proud of.

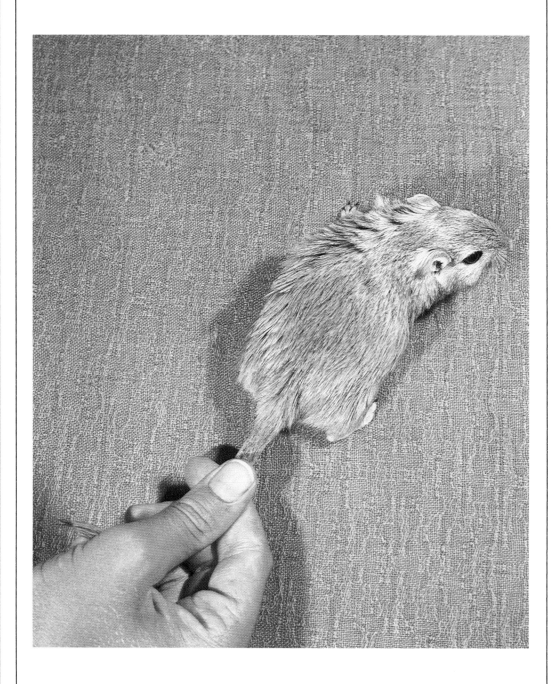

Opposite: Be sure not to let your pet gerbil get near any poisonous plants.

"Some scientists claim that a gerbil mother can get so upset or frightened by loud noises or other disturbances that it will turn on its pups and eat them."

Breeding

Gerbils exhibit different breeding behavior in captivity than in the wilds. Read this chapter carefully if you intend to keep a male-female pair and raise their young — or if the pets you thought were brothers or sisters suddenly present you with a litter. This caution is meant to alert you to a controversial point: Some scientists claim that a gerbil mother can get so upset or frightened by loud noises or other disturbances that it will turn on its pups and eat them.

Other scientists, however, strenuously deny that gerbils could ever do such a thing, no matter how upset or scared they might be. What *can* happen, everyone agrees, is that a startled or upset mother may accidentally trample or suffocate its pups, or desert them to get away from it all.

Another advisory is this: Gerbils can breed so fast that it will make your head spin: Breeders and owners report that within six months, a gerbil pair

A black gerbil mother with her young litter. Gerbil babies don't open their eyes until their third week of life.

It is a good idea to separate the gerbils by sex once they are six weeks old.

"In their desert homes, most litters are born between April and September."

If you plan to add a new gerbil to your collection, you may wish to quarantine it for a few weeks to see that it is in good health.

can produce 25 to 30 animals. Enough said.

In the wilds, gerbil females are receptive to mating only in certain seasons; but in captivity they seem receptive at any time after the age of 3 months and before 20 months.

In their desert homes, most litters are born between April and September. This is sensible, as the pups will have been weaned and on their own while the weather is not too cold and desert vegetation is at its best. A typical gestation period is 24 to 29 days. It can be as long as 45 days if, as often happens, the

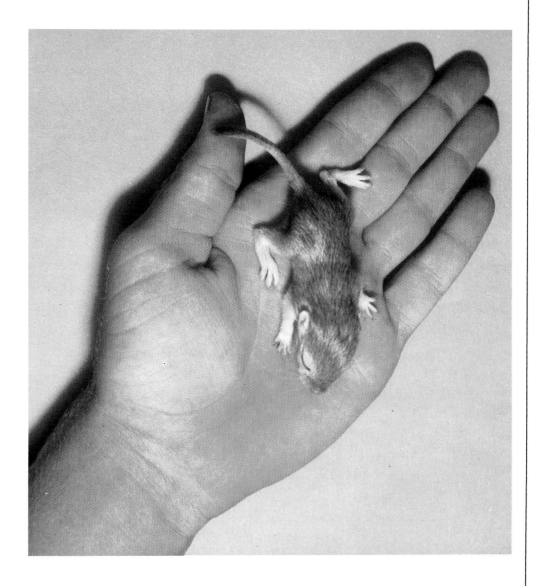

At two weeks of age, the gerbil nearly has its final coloration. However, the eyes are not quite open, and the legs are a bit long.

A pair of gerbils enjoying a sunflower seed snack.

mother becomes pregnant again as soon as her pups are born. The time is longer because gestation is held up until she stops giving milk.

During summers in Mongolia, adult females have litters every 4 to 5 weeks. That's really an assembly line. They can bear pups up to the age of 14 to 20 months. A litter has from 1 to 10 pups, but the average is 3 or 4. Father gerbils usually help care for the young. But even in cases where they keep at a distance, they will not harm the pups. As

A quartet of day-old gerbils. Note their tiny size.

"Pregnant gerbils may become visibly pear-shaped but appear as frisky and agile as ever."

stated before, Mongolian gerbils are monogamous in both the wilds and captivity.

The pups are weaned at 3 weeks or so and can be on their own by 4 weeks of age.

A problem for gerbil owners is that often it's hard to know when gerbils are pregnant. Pregnant gerbils may become visibly pear-shaped but appear as frisky and agile as ever. For all you know they're overeating or the diet is too high in fat. Also, it's easy to miss the weight buildup sometimes because a well-fed furry animal may just look like it has a very thick, rich coat. Suddenly you get the news by hearing tiny squeaking noises,

A veterinarian may be required to determine the sex of a very young gerbil baby.

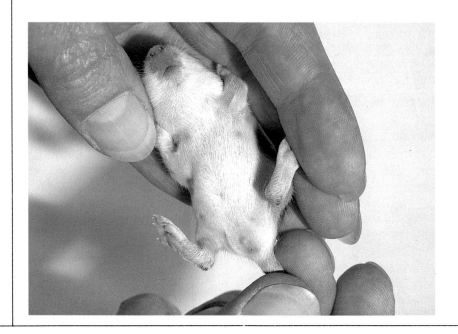

A female black gerbil watching over her one-day-old pups.

The Mating Game

Gerbil matings may be arranged by bringing the couple together before they are sexually mature, at 8 or 9 weeks of age. At this age, they usually have no problem accepting each other. Older gerbils are more fussy about their mates and must be introduced slowly. This is done by keeping them in adjoining enclosures separated by a screen, and hoping they hit it off after a few days. In the wilds, females choose their mates, and the same rule seems to apply among pet gerbils. Females can be very nasty if they don't like the mate you chose for them, and may even attack with intent to kill. This rarely happens, but be careful and be ready to break up a fight.

To be more successful at breeding gerbils, give them some privacy by covering at least one side of the cage or tank with a cloth or cardboard, and eliminate noise or other disturbances. Don't play with them during this time, and make sure they're on a high protein diet.

usually at night or just before dawn, which is when most litters seem to be born. One owner I know discovered a litter only when she was digging away bedding from the water tube. In doing so, she came upon the newborn little wigglers, which the mother had apparently tucked into a nest before going off to rest in a corner. The owner thought she had bought sisters.

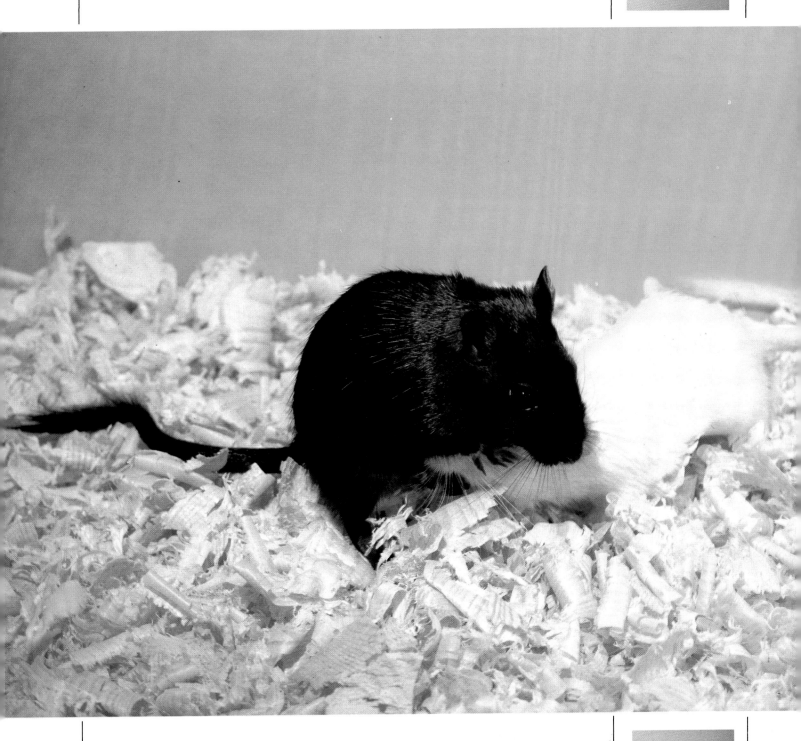

A black gerbil and an albino gerbil.

The mating act is a hectic business. A female in heat will lead the male on a merry chase until the two finally get together. A female will be in heat every 4 to 6 days, but only for about 12 hours each time.

When the female has decided, for whatever reason, to stop running and start a new family, she stops and raises her hindquarters. The male is then able to copulate with her. But this too takes some time. The couple copulate often while she is in heat.

Like other rodents, pregnant gerbils somehow know immediately that they must build a nest for the coming babies. Larger mammals don't display this "nesting" behavior until much closer to birth time. Assuming you know the female is pregnant, you'll want to provide some extra nesting materials,

A dove female gerbil and an agouti Canadian white spot male gerbil just prior to mating.

Many gerbils love eating wool and other materials. Therefore, keep your favorite sweaters and blankets out of their reach.

Opposite: When gerbils are first paired together for the purpose of breeding, they will sniff each other to establish each other's gender.

An Egyptian gerbil mother with her young litter.

such as cotton, wool, cardboard, hay, or whatever. Don't be surprised if the nest looks like a bird's nest and sits atop other bedding. Some owners supply a nesting box, which is just a small wooden shelter about 6 inches on a side, with a roof and a gerbil-size entrance. Mother gerbil will line the box inside with cotton, etc. Papa gerbil often helps out from the start, or lends a hand just before the litter is born.

The Pups Arrive

During birth and just afterward, papa gerbil leaves the nest and beds down in another part of the enclosure. He'll return in a few days and help care for the young. He'll sit on the nest to keep the pups warm and bring back pups who may have strayed. Parents will carry pups in their forepaws or in the mouth.

Warmth is what the pups certainly need, as they're born hairless. About an inch long, they're also deaf, blind (their eyes are closed), toothless, and have no whiskers as yet. Legs and toes are well developed, but the ears are glued back against the head. Still and all, they have the instinct to immediately nuzzle up to mother's belly and drink milk.

Each pup is born easily, wrapped in a shiny membrane. Mother knows exactly what to do. Like so many other animal mothers, she frees the babes from the membrane (the embryonic sac) by chewing the edges and stripping it off. She then eats the placenta (umbilical cord). Keep in mind that gerbils are basically vegetarians. Yet, the mother will eat the placenta, which is a fleshy material, and it's a good thing she does. It provides hormones that help stop

Once two gerbils have paired up, they will become very attached to each other.

An agouti Canadian white spot male gerbil and a dove female gerbil mating.

bleeding caused by birth and also return the womb to its normal size before pregnancy.

You can't help the mother in any way, and you shouldn't try. With her first litter she may be a little unsure of herself, but her instincts generally keep her on the right track. She'll improve with future litters.

After freeing the pups, she licks their bodies in a move scientists believe stimulates the pups to breathe normally. However, recent evidence indicates that even as early as in the womb, mammalian embryos already have begun to breathe. What they're breathing, of course, is the amniotic fluid in which they float while in the womb. (Human embryos even suck their thumb in the womb.) What the mother's vigorous licking may do is help massage the pup's chest and rid its airways of any remaining amniotic fluid.

While still blind — before their eyes open — healthy pups will start squirming almost from

"While still blind — before their eyes open — healthy pups will start squirming almost from birth."

An Egyptian gerbil with its young litter. Although they are fully furred, the babies' eyes are still closed.

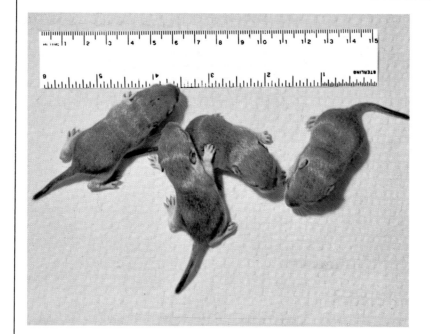

A quartet of two-week-old gerbils. Note how the fur has developed.

Opposite: A dove female gerbil and her litter.

A litter of day old baby gerbils. If possible, do not handle very young gerbils.

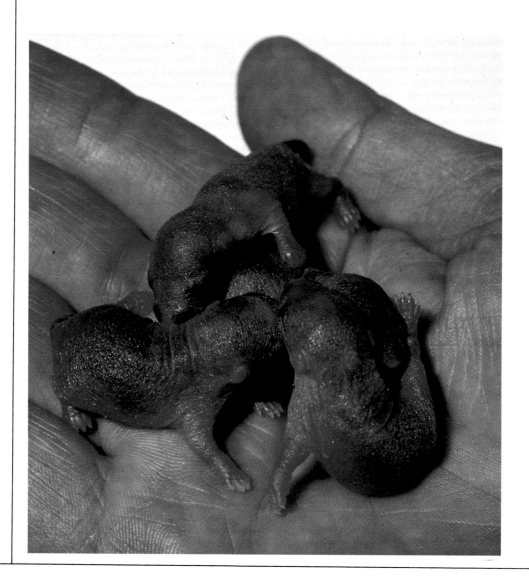

"As with most other mammals, litters sometimes have a runt, an abnormally frail little guy who doesn't feed properly and doesn't get around much."

Opposite: **The mother gerbil may receive help from the father gerbil in raising the litter, but the owner should interfere as little as possible.**

birth. In a day or so they may wriggle out of the nest. The mother licks their bodies after each feeding to stimulate them to pass urine or feces. She licks up all the newborn's waste material to keep the nest clean.

Except for their small size and closed eyes, at about two weeks of age the pups should look like the parents in many respects, including a good fur coat and whiskers. Blind though they may still be, they will be climbing a bit or jumping, and they're easily startled. The eyes open during the third week, and most pups will have their incisors in working order. Now starts the characteristic gnawing. These age figures are only averages.

Some pups take a little longer, some get there faster, so don't be alarmed if the pups don't appear to be progressing according to an exact plan.

As with most other mammals, litters sometimes have a runt, an abnormally frail little guy who doesn't feed properly and doesn't get around much. Runts rarely survive the first week, but if they do they have an excellent chance to make it.

Because they can see, healthy pups should become lots more active. They ought to be capable of sitting up, although shakily for a while, and probably will do some flealike jumps now and then.

At three weeks, the babies can

A trio of baby gerbils. Note the hairlessness of the tails and feet.

A trio of ten-day-old gerbil babies.

**A trio of 15-
day-old
gerbils.**

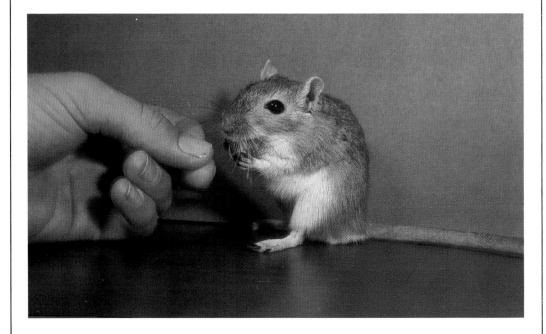

Young, hand-tame gerbils are in great demand as pets. Be sure, however, not to sell a gerbil that is too young to leave its mother.

"To protect the mother's health, the pups should be removed now or in a week to another enclosure. This lets the mother regain her strength more quickly."

eat solid food and drink water from the bottle after some experience with it. They can also drum with their hind legs, although it doesn't seem to have any special purpose at this time. If you don't remove the pups at the end of the third week, the mother will continue nursing them for as long as three more weeks. To protect the mother's health, the pups should be removed now or in a week to another enclosure. This lets the mother regain her strength more quickly. She may need her strength soon, as she may already be pregnant again.

Keep Mother Calm

Some scientists advise not disturbing even a hand-tame mother during or shortly after birth, or the new mom may kill and eat her little ones. Many a litter has been erased this way, according to these authorities. Other scientists, however, point out that they've never seen this terrible thing happen no matter

how upset mother has gotten. They do report that frightened mothers have been known to get into a panic, and in the process stomp the newborns or smother them. The pups also could be hurt if the mother is in heat, and she's crashing around the cage with her mate.

I know several gerbil owners who have handled the newborns as early as the second day after birth with no problem. When the babies were returned, mother washed them down with her tongue. At three to four weeks the pups can be handled for many minutes with no trouble from the mother or father.

The best advice may be: Leave well enough alone. Don't disturb the gerbil family for at least a week.

Bringing Up Baby

To wean pups (at the end of the third week), move them to another cage or tank and provide the same food you give parents. You can now determine their sex — if you're lucky. Some owners we know at first decided this one's a male, that's a female, etc. A few days later they changed their mind...And a few days after, they gave up trying. But after 6 weeks it gets much easier to tell the difference.

If there were runts and they made it this far, you may have to put them in private quarters if their litter mates are pushing them around.

In a typical litter of three or more, you're apt to see some fights. This usually takes the form of a boxing match, punching with their forepaws. Sometimes they seem to wrestle on the floor and take turns locking the other in a jaw hold. Usually, it's not as bad as it looks. Typically, the fight suddenly ends and they engage in a friendly grooming session, licking each other all over. But use your judgment. Break up the fight if it looks serious and goes on too long.

"In a typical litter of three or more, you're apt to see some fights."

A dove female and an agouti Canadian white spot male with their young litter.

A typical gerbil cage will house a pair of gerbils and their young litter comfortably. However, once the young are a few weeks old, they must be moved or the cage will become overcrowded.

Opposite: Note how the different colors of these gerbils are already visible on these youngsters.

The gerbil mother may shred anything she can get her teeth into in order to make a nest for her impending litter.

The Amateur Gerbil Doctor

"Mongolian gerbils are very robust by nature and rarely have health problems."

Observation is a key factor in spotting illness in your pet. Keep an eye out for anything unusual in your pet's behavior or appearance.

Mongolian gerbils are very robust by nature and rarely have health problems. They have no inherited tendencies, as many other animals have, to serious disorders such as cancers or heart disease. Their main problems involve infections by bacteria or upsets due to dietary deficiency.

Whatever the problem your gerbil may have, never use the antibiotic streptomycin to treat it as it has caused many deaths among these animals.

A gerbil problem that does *look* scary, but is quite harmless, is a tendency to epileptic seizures. Only one out of every five gerbils has this tendency. The seizure lasts only a few minutes and the animal returns to normal. Suddenly, the susceptible animal will go limp or lapse into a trance. Some will fall over and kick convulsively. Between evidence gathered by researchers and the experience of gerbil owners, the cause is pretty clear: Seizures may be brought on by any activity that takes the animal out of its familiar surroundings, or even by any rapid change in such conditions as temperature or lighting. As stated above, the condition is harmless and affects only a small percentage of gerbils. It's not caused by diet, infection or overcrowding. The seizure lasts only a minute or two and passes. After a short dizzy spell or seeming to be dazed, the gerbil recovers and seems fine. If it happens to your gerbil, don't try to shake and arouse it. Just pick it up gently and put it in a

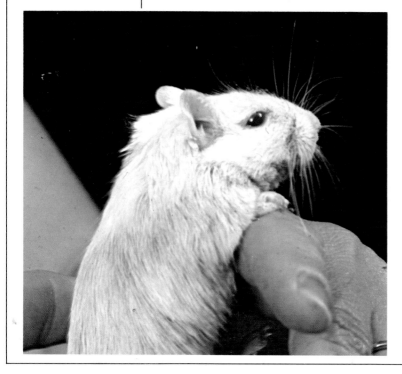

Rumpled fur is not a sure sign of illness. The fur may have been mussed by the gerbil's sleeping position.

A diet consisting of nothing but sunflower seeds is monotonous, no matter how much gerbils love them. In addition, such a diet would be extremely detrimental to the animal's health.

Before breeding any gerbil, be sure that it is in the best of health. If the parents are strong and healthy, chances are the babies will be too.

A coat that is sleek and glossy indicates good health, as does a tail that is free from cuts.

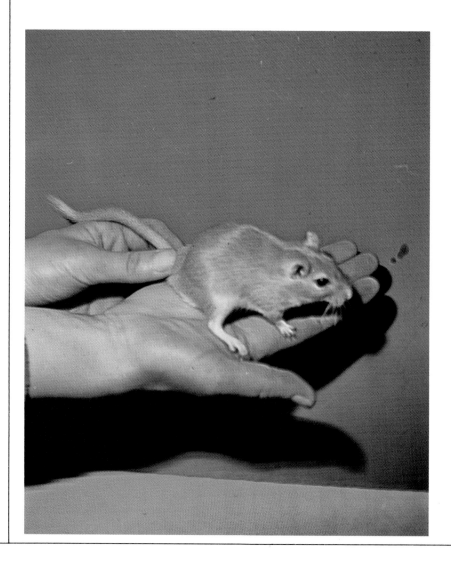

A young dove gerbil at five weeks of age. Note how long the furred tail is by this young age.

Gerbils are notorious gnawers and will chew upon almost anything. Gnawing helps wear away the continuously growing incisors.

Opposite:
Dark and light dove gerbils exploring their surroundings and nibbling on heads of grain.

corner of the cage where it won't be disturbed. If it's outside the cage, bring it back to the cage and let it rest quietly. Usually, other gerbils won't harm it.

Bacterial Diseases

The signs of a serious bacterial infection include diarrhea, rough hair coat, lethargy, appetite loss, and weight loss.

By themselves, lethargy and appetite loss may signal nothing more than a cold. But put it together with diarrhea, or if there's diarrhea alone, your gerbil could have two possible infections: a *Salmonella* infection of the intestines or Tyzzer's disease. *Salmonella* is a bacterium found in spoiled or rotten food. Tyzzer's disease is an infection of the liver and intestinal tract caused by a bacterium of the *Bacillus* type.

There are no specific treatments for either type of infection, although a veterinarian may prescribe an antibiotic that might help.

If the gerbil has only diarrhea, there's no need to rush off to a vet. The problem may be that its food is wet or it's eating too many leafy greens. Try to eliminate these causes and see if it helps. If not, and especially if the gerbil is not eating, take it to a vet.

Intestinal infections with parasitic worms (pinworms, tapeworms) are rare. But even with such infections, gerbils usually show no signs of a problem. You may suspect a parasite if the gerbil is losing weight even though it's eating well. If that's happening, definitely consult a vet.

A nose infection that crops up, appropriately called "red nose," appears as a red, swollen area on the nose and muzzle and may be accompanied by hair loss. The cause is the bacterium *Staphylococcus,* and the infection goes away by itself. It may be hurried along by application of

"By themselves, lethargy and appetite loss may signal nothing more than a cold."

An albino gerbil and a normal gerbil. A healthy gerbil should never be allowed to come into contact with a sick animal.

A wild king gerbil. The diet of the gerbil in captivity should contain the same nutrients the gerbil would find in nature.

an antibiotic salve. A vet may prescribe an antibiotic to be taken in the food.

Sores may appear on the nose following injury due to burrowing or poking the snout through cage bars. A mild antiseptic usually clears it up.

Eye Trouble

Eye inflammations caused by infection should respond to an antibiotic ointment that vets can prescribe. Squeezing the ointment from a tube into the gerbil's eye is a real art, and it may not work at all. You might have better luck by putting a spot of ointment on one of your fingers, holding the animal in the other hand, and using the finger to dab the stuff on. An eye infection that doesn't respond may require a bacterial culture to identify the organism and determine which antibiotic is best for it.

A culture may indicate the inflammation is not an infection

An agouti
Canadian
white spot
gerbil that is
clearly
interested in
something—
the camera,
perhaps?

after all. In that case, the animal could be allergic to the bedding or something else in the cage. Some authorities believe it might be due to a dietary deficiency — not enough fresh fruits or vegetables. You can try a change of bedding or beefing up the diet with fresh food.

thorough investigation of the cause.

Finally, three or four-year old gerbils often contract an eye condition of unknown cause, in which one or both eyes bulge and the eyelid inflames. There's no cure, but no visual impairment occurs.

Gerbil working its way through a maze of brightly colored blocks. To keep your pet healthy, be sure he gets a chance to exercise regularly.

"Poor diet can lead to hair loss, shaggy coat, a wobbly gait, and weight loss."

There are still other cases of eye inflammation caused by the animal's continual scratching or overly eager grooming. And sometimes the cause is a mystery; the inflammation may disappear, but the eye(s) remain swollen — the lids almost shut tight — and the gerbil eats less and loses some weight. The resolution of this problem could require repeated visits to a vet for a

Nutritional Deficiency

Poor diet can lead to hair loss, shaggy coat, a wobbly gait, and weight loss. Often, the problem is a deficiency of B vitamins. It is easily treated with multivitamin drops in the dry food and in the water.

Gerbils In The Laboratory

The subject of gerbils as laboratory animals is not a

If you must hold your gerbil by its tail, secure it by the base of the tail, not the tip; do not hold your pet this way for more than a few seconds.

A homemade obstacle course. If you have any doubt about the safety of the household items your pet plays with, take them away and provide a safe toy from your pet shop.

Note the bright, clear, alert eyes on this little fellow.

A gerbil poking its nose out of a traveling cage. Such a cage is a must if you plan to travel with your pet.

Some gerbils love to scatter their meals around the cage before eating. Do not be alarmed if your pet indulges in this behavior.

Opposite: **Gerbils are among the healthiest rodents, as they are subject to very few diseases and disorders.**

favorite of gerbil lovers. In a way, it's sad to think of the endearing creatures as often penned up in small cages, given various diseases in order to find cures, and generally leading an abnormal life, far from any home

Some gerbils are subject to brief seizures which are considered epileptic in nature. These seizures do not seem to produce any after-effects.

". . .Mongolian gerbils had the bad luck of being good research subjects for two reasons: they're so easy and inexpensive to maintain; and they have certain bodily characteristics making them ideal for experiments. . ."

or family. On the other hand, animals such as gerbils are required in medical research if we are to save human beings from the ravages of disease. It's something animal lovers must accept, not only where gerbils are involved, but many other species as well. But we must be sure that our laboratory animals are treated humanely, as far as this is possible. This means they should be free of pain and not used in unnecessary experiments that cause suffering with no useful purpose to humankind.

As far as medical research goes, you may say Mongolian gerbils had the bad luck of being good research subjects for two reasons: they're so easy and inexpensive to maintain; and, they have certain bodily characteristics making them ideal for experiments that could tell us how to prevent or cure

Aging gerbils have a tendency to become overweight. Their food intake should be restricted somewhat, but the quality of the diet should remain high. Ask your veterinarian about the proper way to put your gerbil on a diet.

Three types of rodents: a gerbil, a rat, and a mouse. Note the differences in physicality and expression.

Gerbils may not be as diligent about running through mazes for a reward as are mice and rats, but this does not mean they are not intelligent. Gerbils are simply more curious and are not as single-minded as other rodents.

When breeding young gerbils, keep in mind that all gerbils are individuals and have different rates of progress.

Right: A blue gerbil. Blue is a relatively rare color in gerbils. *Far right:* A chinchilla gerbil.

Right: A cinnamon white spot gerbil keeping a lookout while his pal, an agouti, explores under a rock. *Far right:* A gray gerbil taking a lunch break.

serious human disorders. The disorders include epileptic seizures, heart disease, and a form of cancer called melanoma. Moreover, gerbils could be more useful than any other lab animal for studies of organ transplants as well as resistance to nuclear radiation.

Epilepsy

No other lab animal suffers the type of seizure that affects some gerbils. Yet the seizures do resemble those that occur in humans with epilepsy. Human epilepsy is caused by a brain dysfunction that may cause loss of consciousness or convulsive movements of various parts of the body.

Working with seizure-prone gerbils, researchers implant electrodes in the animal's brain and record the brain's electrical activity. (This isn't painful for the animal.) Then, by producing the situations that often cause

Most gerbils do not overeat most foods, but they do tend to overdo the sunflower seeds. Therefore, it is not a good idea to leave sunflower seeds in reach of your gerbils too often.

seizures in gerbils, they can study the difference between the animal's normal brain activity and its activity during seizures. Researchers can use gerbils to test new drugs for epileptics because they have found that drugs which prevent human seizures also prevent gerbil seizures.

In experiments with such gerbils, researchers found that gerbil seizures could be caused by handling, sudden temperature or lighting changes, or by placing the animal in an unfamiliar environment.

Breeding gerbils can be a rewarding experience if it is gone about with the health and safety of the gerbils in mind. Pet gerbils are now available in several colors and varieties.

". . .researchers found that gerbil seizures could be caused by handling, sudden temperature or lighting changes, or by placing the animal in an unfamiliar environment."

Gerbils are adorable when eating out of your hand. A responsible pet owner must resist the temptation to overfeed his gerbil in this manner.

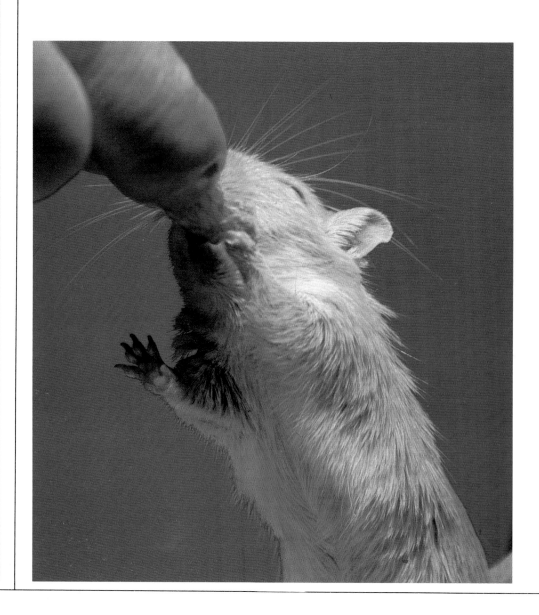

A striking
black gerbil.

A gerbil in the act of marking its territory. This activity looks very strange when you see it for the first time.

Heart Disease

Heart specialists believe that a major cause of heart attacks is the buildup in the bloodstream of cholesterol, a fatty substance that can clog the arteries and block bloodflow to the heart. When that type of block occurs, the heart muscle becomes "starved" for oxygen and cannot pump blood to the brain and other vital organs. Gerbils are especially useful in heart research because they never develop the fatty blockages that cause heart attacks, even though they have very large amounts of cholesterol in their blood. People with high cholesterol often do develop blocked arteries — but why don't gerbils? If we discover the answer to this question, it may lead us to methods for preventing human heart attacks.

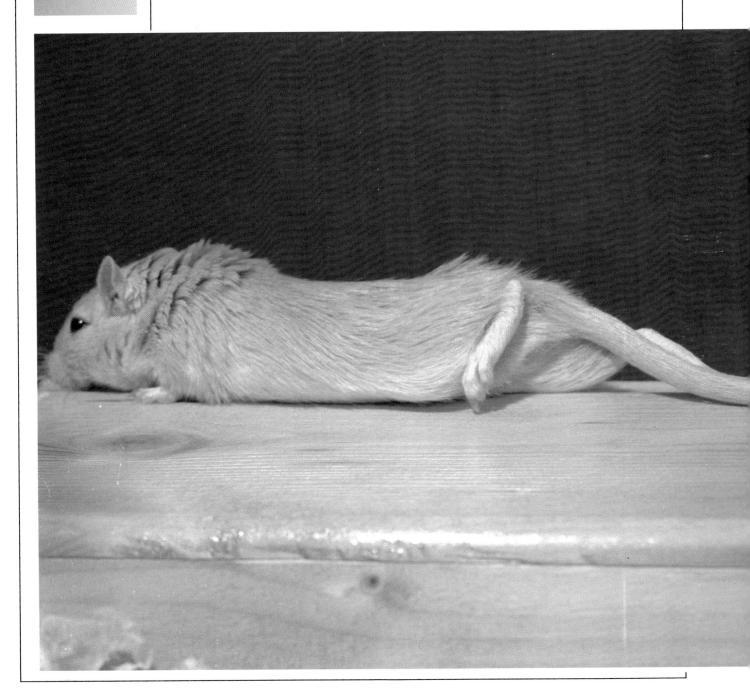

Paired gerbils grow very attached to each other; when one member of the pair dies, the other may mourn for it for months.

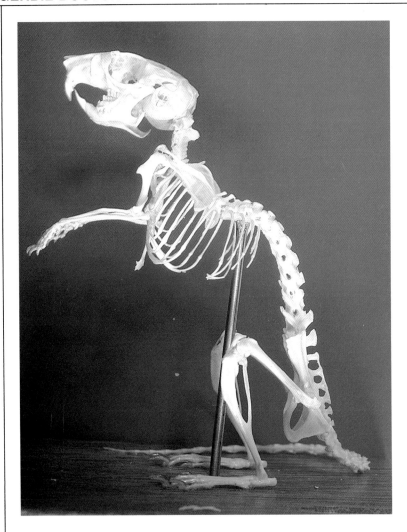

Skeleton of a gerbil. Since the gerbil is a healthy animal with several physiological similarities to humans, it has been used as a laboratory animal.

A gerbil and a mouse that have been raised together. Gerbils usually do well on diets that have been formulated for mice.

A trio of baby gerbils getting ready to encounter the outside world.

No matter what you're doing, your pet gerbil will want to know what's going on.

Opposite: A pair of gerbils rearranging their quarters to suit their moods.

Melanoma

Melanoma, a cancer that may develop in the skin of any part of the body, develops from those cells that are capable of making a dark pigment called melanin. (When we get suntanned, the tan color is caused by the accumulation of melanin in the skin. The dark coloration of moles also is due to melanin.) As far back as 1947, an Air Force sergeant named Norman W. Olsen first sparked the idea of using black gerbils for cancer research. As you can imagine, here is a gerbil overloaded with melanin-producing cells. With the help of D.G. Robinson of Tumblebrook Farm, Sergeant Olsen succeeded in breeding black mutant gerbils for the first time.

This is the most secure grip to use when you are checking your gerbil for signs of ill health or injury.

Organ Transplants

You're probably familiar with the fact that, for many years, surgeons have been able to transplant a kidney from a donor individual to a person whose kidneys do not work at all and who would die without the new kidney. Heart transplants are more in the limelight and in the news. In both instances, the major problem is not in hooking up the new organ, but in keeping the recipient's body from "rejecting" and destroying the foreign tissue. The rejection is caused by a mechanism in every individual's immune system which recognizes that a transplanted organ does not belong to the "self" and therefore must be destroyed. Kidney transplants have fewest problems of this kind when the donor and recipient are very close relatives (a brother, sister, etc.). In such cases the recipient's immune system does not go into the destructive panic and treat the new organ as a foreign invader. Hence no rejection occurs.

"Kidney transplants have fewest problems of this kind when the donor and recipient are very close relatives. . ."

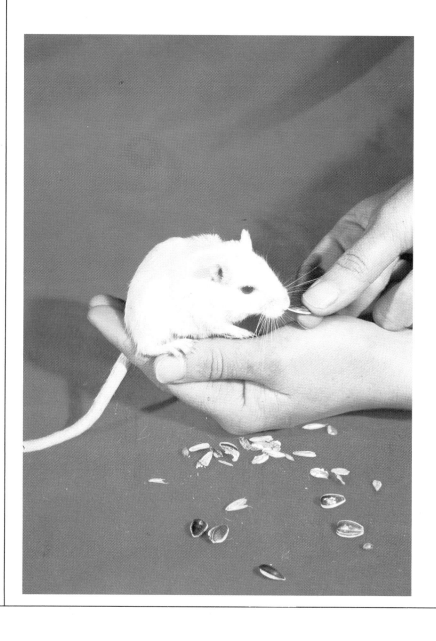

An albino gerbil getting a reward of sunflower seeds. If your gerbil isn't interested in his usual favorites, a trip to the vet might be in order.

A trio of gerbils eating and exploring, two of their favorite pastimes.

A black gerbil going down. Climbing is a favorite activity of many gerbils.

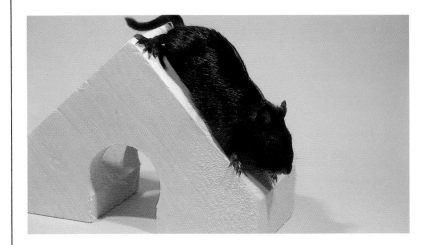

A pair of agouti gerbils saying hello.

The importance of a nutritious diet cannot be overstressed. A well-balanced, interestingly varied diet will keep your pet healthy and alert.

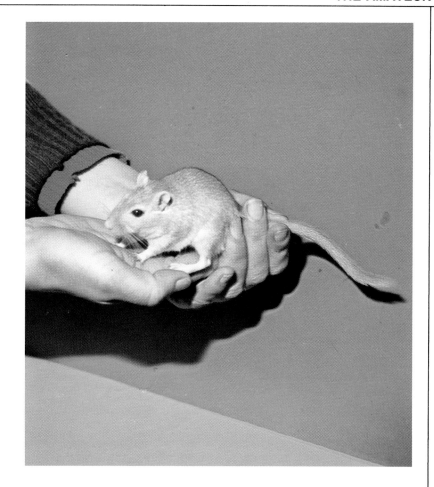

A pet gerbil exploring its master's hand. It probably has an idea about running up the owner's sleeve.

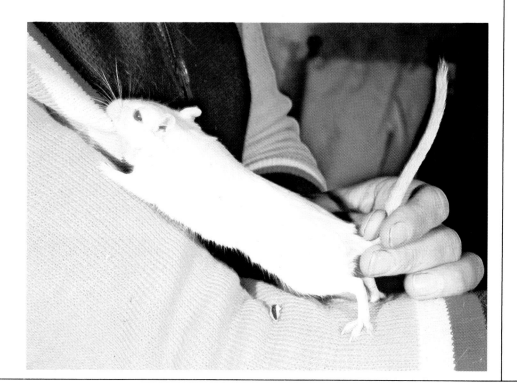

The strong hind legs and feet of this gerbil are clearly visible. Gerbils are sturdy little creatures that will usually climb wherever they can.

A gerbil in an exhibition cage. An exhibition cage is not nearly big enough to be suitable for traveling with your pet gerbil.

". . . [Gerbils and hamsters] are the only small mammals we know of that don't reject tissue transplants from other animals . . ."

In all other cases, recipients must depend on taking drugs that block the immune system from reacting. Once again, gerbils enter the picture. They and hamsters have a unique characteristic: They are the only small mammals we know of that don't reject tissue transplants from other animals (of the same species, of course). You'd think that such animals would have abnormal immune systems — but they do very well otherwise in protecting themselves from infections and other invaders. For this reason, researchers are studying how the gerbil's immune system works in terms of recognizing tissues that belong to the "self" as opposed to another animal. That knowledge may be applied to improving the outlook for human organ transplants.

A gerbil making its way through a maze. Be sure to use safe, non-toxic blocks if you plan to create a maze for your pet.

A pair of gerbils in their cage. A sick gerbil will often be irritable with cagemates and owner alike.

An agouti male gerbil and a cinnamon female gerbil being introduced for the first time.

Some gerbils will wrestle each other for fun. However, if you have recently introduced one gerbil to another (especially if both animals are males), be sure to keep an eye on them for a few days to see that they get along.

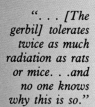

". . . [The gerbil] tolerates twice as much radiation as rats or mice. . .and no one knows why this is so."

Opposite: **A mating pair of gerbils. Be sure that all gerbils you plan to breed are fully matured. Gerbils that are too young will produce inferior offspring.**

Gerbil standing at attention.

Resistance To Radiation

Here again, the gerbil is unusual: It tolerates twice as much radiation as rats or mice — the other most popular lab animals — and no one knows why this is so. One clue is diet. Several studies have suggested that gerbils given their natural diet of seeds, leaves, etc., are more tolerant to radiation than gerbils fed the usual lab chow. If this is the case, then the factor in the diet responsible for the higher tolerance might be used to make humans more tolerant. The most important application of this research is not military — as in protecting humans from nuclear fallout — but in making cancer patients more tolerant to higher doses of therapeutic radiation.

Suggested Reading

GERBILS: A COMPLETE INTRODUCTION
By Mrs. M. Ostrow

Soft cover: **CO-018S** ISBN 0-86622-299-5
All of the basics of good care, management, and breeding of these playful little rodents are presented in tandem with photos that show the different color varieties available.
5½ x 8½ inches, 128 pages.
Contains 93 full-color photos and eight full-color line drawings.

A gerbil farmhouse. Individual gerbils will have their favorite toys.

A STEP-BY-STEP BOOK ABOUT GERBILS
By Patrick Bradley and Heather Spence

Soft cover: ISBN 0-86622-467-X
TFH SK-011
The wonderful, educational world of gerbils can be explored by readers of this step-by-step book. This magnificently colorful book combines full-color humorous drawings with lavish full-color photography—which makes this book as enjoyable to look at as it is to read.
Contents: Introduction. Gerbils As Pets. Handling Gerbils. Housing. Nutritional Needs. Breeding. Illness. Summary. Suggested Reading. Index.
Hard or soft cover, over 50 full-color photos and drawings, 5½ × 8½ inches, 64 pages.

GERBILS
By Paul Paradise
ISBN 0-87666-927-5
TFH KW-037
Updated edition of the durable, information-packed gerbil member of the KW series. This book presents sensible, easy-to-follow recommendations about selecting and caring for the popular Mongolian gerbil in an interesting and understandable style.
Contents: Introduction. What Are Gerbils? The Mongolian Gerbil. Gerbil Maintenance. Gerbil Health. Breeding Your Gerbils. Index.
Hard cover, 5½ × 8 inches, 96 pages, completely illustrated with full-color photographs and drawings.

Index

An albino gerbil and a black gerbil—opposites attract.

Keeping and Breeding Gerbils
TS-120

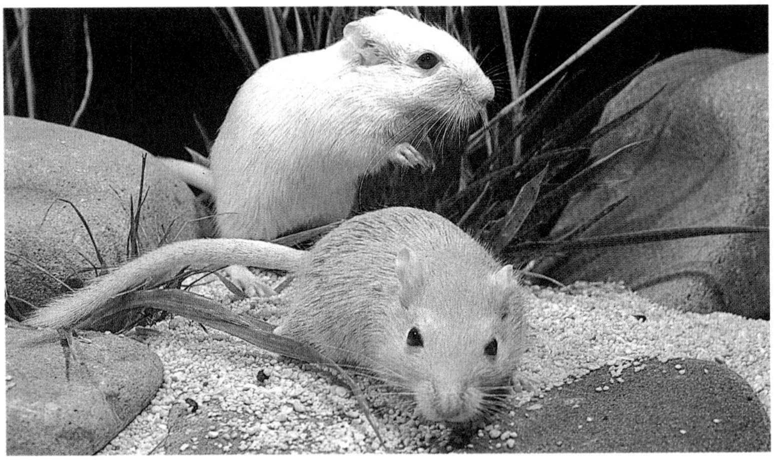